I0833522

Meet the Presidents

Meet the Presidents: An Introduction to the Leaders of the United States

MIKE BLACK

DEDICATION

To my mother, who instilled in me a deep appreciation and fascination for the rich history of the United States of America. Your passion for teaching U.S. history inspired me to delve deeper into the lives and legacies of our nation's presidents. This book is a tribute to your unwavering dedication to education and the impact you have had on countless students, including me. Thank you for sparking my lifelong love of learning and for shaping the person I am today. I dedicate this book to you with all my love and gratitude.

CONTENTS

INTRODUCTION

We designed this book for readers of all ages, but particularly for those in grades 3 to 7.

Do you know who was the first President of the United States? Who was the tallest president? Who was the only president to serve two non-consecutive terms? Who was the first president to live in the White House? What did some presidents do for fun? In this book, you will find the answers to these questions and many more interesting facts about the 46 men who have held the Office of the President of the United States.

Each chapter of this book features a different president, in chronological order, starting with George Washington, who served as the first president from 1789 to 1797, and ending with Joe Biden, who was inaugurated on January 20, 2021. For each president, you will find a brief biography, highlighting their major accomplishments and challenges during their time in office.

Besides their biographies, you will learn about some fun and weird facts about each president. For example, did you know that John Quincy Adams used to go skinny-dipping in the Potomac River every day? Or that Andrew Johnson was a tailor before he became a politician? Or that Jimmy Carter once reported a UFO sighting? These little-known facts will help you get to know the presidents in a different light, and perhaps spark your curiosity to learn more.

As you read through the book, you will also learn about some of the key events and challenges that the United States faced during each president's time in office. For example, you will learn about the American Revolution and the Civil War, as well as other important events like the Great Depression and World War II. You will also learn about some of the major policy initiatives that each president pursued, such as the New Deal, the Civil Rights Act, and the Affordable Care Act.

One goal of this book is to help readers understand the significance of the presidency and the role of the president in shaping American history. The book also aims to encourage readers to think critically about the choices that each president made, and the impact that those choices had on the country and the world.

Whether you are a history buff or just learning about the presidents, "Meet the Presidents: An Introduction to the Leaders of the United States" is a great resource for anyone who wants to learn more about the men who have led the United States throughout its history. So grab a copy, settle in, and get ready to explore the fascinating world of the presidency!

CHAPTER 1

FEDERALIST ERA (1792–1824)

The First Party System was a period in American politics that lasted from 1792 to 1824, and the two dominant political parties of the era: the Federalist Party and the Democratic-Republican Party characterized it. The Federalist Era refers specifically to the period during which the Federalist Party was in power, from 1792 until 1800.

Here is a chronology of the key events within the Federalist Era:

- 1789: George Washington inaugurated as the first President of the United States. The country is governed under the newly ratified Constitution, which was written the previous year.
- 1790: The United States capital moves from New York City to Philadelphia.
- 1791: Congress creates The Bank of the United States at the urging of Secretary of the Treasury Alexander Hamilton, a leading Federalist. This sparked debate over the role of the federal government in the economy and the balance of power between the states and the national government.
- 1792: The first presidential election is held under the Constitution, with George Washington running unopposed and winning a second term. Alexander Hamilton and other supporters of a strong central government found the Federalist Party.
- 1793: France declares war on Great Britain, and the United States declares its neutrality in the conflict. This sparked debate over whether the U.S. should support France, its ally in the American Revolution, or remain neutral.
- 1794: The Whiskey Rebellion, a protest against a tax on whiskey, is put down by state militia, with federal troops providing support. This showed the power of the federal government to enforce its laws and maintain order.
- 1796: John Adams, a Federalist, elected as the second President of the United States. His vice president is Thomas Jefferson, a Democratic-Republican.
- 1797: The XYZ Affair, a diplomatic incident between the U.S. and France, threatens to drag the two countries into war. The Federalists call for a powerful response, while the Democratic-Republicans advocate for negotiation.
- 1800: Thomas Jefferson, a Democratic-Republican, elected as the third President of the United States, defeating incumbent John Adams. This marks the end of the Federalist Era and the beginning of a new period of Democratic-Republican dominance in American politics.

During the Federalist Era, the Federalist Party advocated for a strong central government, a national bank, a standing army, and close ties with Great Britain. They believed that the government should play an active role in the economy and that the states should have limited power. The Democratic-Republicans favored a weaker federal government, state sovereignty, and close ties with France. They believed that the government should play a limited role in the economy and that the states should have more power.

The Federalist Era was a time of great debate over the role of government in American society, and it set the stage for the political divisions that would shape American politics for decades to come.

G. Washington

NICKNAME: "Father of His Country," "The American Cincinnatus," "The Indispensable Man," "The Hero of the Hudson," "The Marble Man," "The Sage of Mount Vernon," and "The Great Unifier"
BORN: February 22, 1732, in Westmoreland County, Virginia
POLITICAL PARTY: Unaffiliated
TERM OF OFFICE: April 30, 1789 – March 4, 1797
VICE PRESIDENT: John Adams
AGE AT INAUGURATION: 57 years
NUMBER OF TERMS: Two full terms
PARENTS:
Augustine Washington
Mary Ball Washington
MARRIED: Martha Dandridge Custis Washington (1732-1802), on January 6, 1759
CHILDREN: John "Jack" Parke Custis (adopted); Martha "Patsy" Custis (adopted)
PETS: Snipe the parrot; 36 hounds; horses
EDUCATION: No formal education
RELIGION: Episcopalian
OCCUPATION: Planter, soldier, public official
OTHER GOVERNMENT POSITIONS: Member of Virginia House of Burgesses, 1759-74; Member of Continental Congress, 1774-75; Chairman of the Constitutional Convention, 1787-88
MILITARY SERVICE: Colonel, Virginia Militia (1752-1758); General and Commander in Chief, Continental Army (1775-1783); Lieutenant General, U.S. Army (1798-1799)
PRESIDENTIAL SALARY: $25,000/year (refused by Washington)
DIED: December 14, 1799, at Mount Vernon, Virginia
AGE AT DEATH: 67 years
CAUSE OF DEATH: Throat Infection
BURIED: Fairfax County, Virginia

George Washington

1st President of the United States (1789 – 1797)

George Washington was a Virginia planter and soldier who became a central figure in the American Revolution and the newly formed United States of America. Before becoming involved in politics, Washington served as a surveyor in Virginia and later fought in the French and Indian War.

During the American Revolution, Washington played a key role in leading the Continental Army to victory against the British. He commanded the army during some of the most crucial battles, including the Battle of Trenton, the Battle of Princeton, and the Battle of Yorktown. His leadership and perseverance were crucial in securing American independence.

After the war, Washington became a prominent figure in the founding of the United States. He presided over the Constitutional Convention in 1787 and played a key role in the drafting of the U.S. Constitution. He was unanimously elected as the first President of the United States in 1789 and served two terms in office.

During his presidency, Washington established many important precedents, including the tradition of delivering an inaugural address, the use of the title "Mr. President," and the creation of a presidential cabinet. He also signed into law the Judiciary Act of 1789, which established the federal court system.

We also know Washington for his Farewell Address, delivered at the end of his second term, in which he emphasized the importance of national unity and warned against the dangers of political parties and foreign entanglements.

Throughout his life, George Washington was admired for his leadership, integrity, and dedication to his country. People remember him as a figure of great respect in American history and often refer to him as the "Father of His Country."

Fun Facts:

- George Washington never lived in the White House: Although he was the first President of the United States, Washington never lived in the White House. They did not complete the building until after his death.
- He had a set of false teeth made of various materials, including lead, ivory, human teeth, and animal teeth.
- He was the first person to sign the U.S. Constitution.
- George Washington is the only person to have been unanimously elected as U.S. president.
- The surprise attack carried out by Lieutenant Colonel George Washington of the Virginia Regiment against a small French force at Jumonville Glen in 1754, followed by his surrender to French forces at the Battle of Fort Necessity, played a role in igniting the French and Indian War. This conflict was part of the larger imperial struggle between Great Britain and France, also known as the Seven Years' War.
- He was a successful whiskey distiller: After leaving the presidency, Washington went into business as a whiskey distiller. His distillery at Mount Vernon was one of the largest in the country at the time and produced up to 12,000 gallons of whiskey per year.
- Despite wigs being in fashion, George Washington kept his own hair.
- Washington's favorite breakfast dish was hoecakes, which were made from cornmeal, water, and salt and cooked on a griddle.

John Adams

NICKNAME: "Atlas of Independence," "Father of the American Navy," "Old Sink or Swim," "His Rotundity," "The Colossus of Independence," "The Duke of Braintree," "The Massachusetts Cincinnatus," and "The Puritan President"
BORN: October 30, 1735, in Braintree (now Quincy), Massachusetts
POLITICAL PARTY: Federalist
TERM OF OFFICE: March 4, 1797 – March 4, 1801
VICE PRESIDENT: Thomas Jefferson
AGE AT INAUGURATION: 61 years
NUMBER OF TERMS: One full term
PARENTS:
John Adams
Susanna Boylston Adams
MARRIED: Abigail Smith Adams (1744-1818), on October 25, 1764
CHILDREN: Abigail, John Quincy, Susanna, Charles, Thomas
PETS: mixed-breed dogs named Juno and Satan, and horses named Caesar and Cleopatra
EDUCATION: Graduated from Harvard College (1755)
RELIGION: Unitarian
OCCUPATION: Lawyer, public official
OTHER GOVERNMENT POSITIONS: Member of Continental Congress, 1774-78; Commissioner to France, 1778; Minister to the Netherlands, 1780; Minister to England, 1785; Vice President, 1789-97 (under Washington)
MILITARY SERVICE: None
PRESIDENTIAL SALARY: $25,000/year
DIED: July 4, 1826, in Braintree (now Quincy), Massachusetts
AGE AT DEATH: 90 years
CAUSE OF DEATH: Heart Attack
BURIED: Quincy, Massachusetts

John Adams

2nd President of the United States (1797 – 1801)

John Adams was a Founding Father of the United States and a key figure in the American Revolution. Prior to becoming President, he played a significant role in the early history of the United States.

Before his presidency, Adams was a leading advocate for colonial independence from Britain. He was a member of the Continental Congress and served on several committees, including the committee that drafted the Declaration of Independence. He also served as an ambassador to France and the Netherlands, where he negotiated important treaties and secured much-needed loans for the fledgling United States.

During his presidency, Adams faced numerous challenges, including tensions with France, which led to the Quasi-War, a naval conflict between the United States and France. Adams also signed the Alien and Sedition Acts, which were controversial laws that made it more difficult for immigrants to become citizens and restricted freedom of speech and the press.

Despite these challenges, Adams made several important accomplishments during his presidency. He appointed John Marshall as Chief Justice of the Supreme Court, which helped to establish the independence and authority of the judicial branch of government. John Adams established the Department of the Navy while he was serving as president and oversaw the launch of several ships including the U.S.S. Constitution.

Overall, John Adams was a key figure in the early history of the United States and played an important role in the country's founding and early development.

Fun Facts:

- John Adams and Thomas Jefferson both died on July 4, 1826, the 50th anniversary of the signing of the Declaration of Independence.
- Adams was the only president to be elected as a Federalist, a party that believed in a strong central government and a national bank. He was also the only president to serve as Vice President under George Washington.
- Adams was a prolific writer and kept diaries for much of his life. His diaries provided valuable insights into the political and social climate of his time.
- Adams was known for his sharp tongue and was prone to outbursts of anger. He famously called his political rival Alexander Hamilton "the bastard brat of a Scottish peddler."
- He defended the British soldiers who were involved in the Boston Massacre, arguing that they deserved a fair trial.
- John Adams was the first president to be related to another president. His son, John Quincy Adams, served as the sixth president of the United States.
- Adams stood out among the founding fathers for not owning slaves, but he did not actively advocate for abolitionism. However, he did express that he would only support gradual abolition with great care and caution.
- Adams had a pet dog named "Satan," which he reportedly enjoyed playing with.
- He and his wife Abigail were the first presidential couple to live in the White House, and Abigail was known for her sharp wit and her letters to her husband.

W. Jefferson

NICKNAME: "Father of the Declaration of Independence"
BORN: April 13, 1743, in Shadwell, Virginia
POLITICAL PARTY: Democratic-Republican
TERM OF OFFICE: (March 4, 1801 – March 3, 1809)
VICE PRESIDENT: Aaron Burr (1801– 1805), George Clinton (1805-1812)
AGE AT INAUGURATION: 57 years
NUMBER OF TERMS: Two full terms
PARENTS:
Peter Jefferson
Jane Randolph Jefferson
MARRIED: Martha Wayles Skelton Jefferson (1748-1782), on January 1, 1772
CHILDREN: With Martha Jefferson: Martha, Jane, Mary, Lucy, Lucy II, unnamed son; Alleged children with Sally Hemings (one of his slaves): Thomas, Harriet, Edy, William, Thenia, Harriet II, James, Eston
PETS: a mockingbird; 2 bear cubs
EDUCATION: Graduated from College of William and Mary (1762)
RELIGION: No formal affiliation
OCCUPATION: Lawyer, planter,
OTHER GOVERNMENT POSITIONS: Member of Virginia House of Burgesses, 1769-74; Member of Continental Congress, 1775-76; Governor of Virginia, 1779-81; Member of Continental Congress, 1783-85; Minister to France, 1785-89; Secretary of State, 1790-93 (under Washington); Vice President, 1797-1801 (under J. Adams)
MILITARY SERVICE: Colonel, Virginia Militia (1770-1779)
PRESIDENTIAL SALARY: $25,000/year
DIED: July 4, 1826, at Monticello
AGE AT DEATH: 83 years
CAUSE OF DEATH: Cancer
BURIED: Charlottesville, Virginia

Thomas Jefferson

3rd President of the United States (1801 – 1809)

Thomas Jefferson was born in Virginia in 1743 and was the third child of ten siblings. He grew up in a family that valued education, and he received an excellent education from private tutors and at the College of William and Mary.

Jefferson's accomplishments before his presidency include serving as a member of the Virginia House of Burgesses, where he became known for his support of individual rights and opposition to British colonial policies. He also served in the Continental Congress and was the principal author of the Declaration of Independence, which he drafted in 1776.

During his presidency, Jefferson accomplished a great deal. He oversaw the Louisiana Purchase, which doubled the size of the United States, and he also established the United States Military Academy at West Point. Jefferson also signed the Embargo Act of 1807, which sought to avoid American involvement in European conflicts by banning all trade with foreign countries.

Besides his political accomplishments, Jefferson was also an accomplished writer and philosopher. He authored several influential works, including "Notes on the State of Virginia" and the "Jefferson Bible," which reinterpreted the Gospels to focus on the moral teachings of Jesus.

Despite his many accomplishments, Jefferson was not without controversy. He was a slave owner who spoke out against the practice of slavery, but never took significant action to abolish it. He also had a complicated relationship with religion, and his views on the subject were often the subject of criticism.

Overall, however, Thomas Jefferson remains one of the most important and influential figures in American history, whose ideas and legacy continue to shape the country to this day.

Fun Facts:

- Thomas Jefferson was a lifelong inventor and tinkerer. He designed a revolving bookstand, a macaroni machine, and an improved plow.
- He was a fan of vanilla ice cream, and brought the recipe to the United States after tasting it in France.
- Jefferson was a prolific writer, and his written output includes over 18,000 letters, multiple books, and even the design for his own tombstone.
- He spoke six languages: English, French, Italian, Spanish, Latin, and Greek.
- Jefferson was an early advocate for the use of vaccinations to prevent disease. He even had his own family vaccinated against smallpox.
- He kept pet mockingbirds and even allowed them to fly freely around his home.
- He was an avid reader and owned a personal library of over 6,000 books. When the Library of Congress was burned during the War of 1812, Jefferson offered to sell his personal library to the government to help rebuild it.
- Jefferson supported limited federal power and decentralized government. However, during his presidency, he approved the Louisiana Purchase, which doubled the size of the United States.
- He invented a bookstand that let him read up to five books simultaneously.

James Madison (signature)

NICKNAME: "Father of the Constitution," "The American Cicero," "Little Jemmy," and "The American Cicero,"
BORN: March 16, 1751, in Port Conway, Virginia
POLITICAL PARTY: Democratic-Republican
TERM OF OFFICE: (March 4, 1809 – March 3, 1817)
VICE PRESIDENT: George Clinton (1805–1812), Elbridge Gerry (1813–1814)
AGE AT INAUGURATION: 57 years
NUMBER OF TERMS: Two full terms
PARENTS:
James Madison
Nelly Conway Madison
MARRIED: Dolley Payne Todd Madison (1768-1849), on September 15, 1794
CHILDREN: Stepchildren John and William
PETS: Macaw the parrot; sheep
EDUCATION: Graduated from College of New Jersey (now Princeton University; 1771)
RELIGION: Episcopalian
OCCUPATION: Lawyer, public official
OTHER GOVERNMENT POSITIONS: Member of Virginia Constitutional Convention, 1776; Member of Continental Congress, 1780-83; Member of Virginia Legislature, 1784-86; Member of Constitutional Convention, 1787; Member of U.S. House of Representatives, 1789-97; Secretary of State, 1801-09 (under Jefferson)
MILITARY SERVICE: Colonel, Virginia Militia (1775-1781)
PRESIDENTIAL SALARY: $25,000/year
DIED: June 28, 1836, at Montpelier, Virginia
AGE AT DEATH: 85 years
CAUSE OF DEATH: Heart Failure
BURIED: Orange, Virginia

James Madison

4th President of the United States (1809 – 1817)

James Madison was born in Port Conway, Virginia, and grew up on a plantation in Orange County, Virginia. He was the oldest of twelve children and received his early education from private tutors. Madison's father was a wealthy tobacco planter and served as a justice of the peace and county sheriff.

Madison was a brilliant student, particularly in languages and history. He studied at the College of New Jersey (now Princeton University), where John Witherspoon, a signer of the Declaration of Independence, deeply influenced him. Madison's studies at Princeton included a focus on politics and government, and he became deeply committed to the cause of American independence.

During his presidency, Madison accomplished several significant achievements, including the successful prosecution of the War of 1812 against Britain. He also oversaw the expansion of the United States through the acquisition of Louisiana from France in 1803 and the annexation of West Florida from Spain in 1811.

Madison is perhaps best known for his role in drafting the United States Constitution, and he played a critical role in the document's ratification by leading the effort to secure the passage of the Bill of Rights. As a member of the House of Representatives, Madison authored the Virginia Plan, which served as the basis for the Constitution.

After his presidency, Madison continued to be involved in politics and public service. He was a powerful advocate for religious freedom and served as Rector of the University of Virginia, which was founded by his friend and fellow Founding Father, Thomas Jefferson. Madison also worked tirelessly to promote education and civic participation, believing that an informed and engaged citizenry was essential to the success of the young nation.

Throughout his life, James Madison showed a deep commitment to the principles of democracy and the rule of law. His contributions to American politics and government continue to be felt today, and his legacy as one of the Founding Fathers of the United States remains secure.

Fun Facts:

- James Madison was the shortest U.S. president, standing at only 5 feet 4 inches tall.
- He was the primary author of the U.S. Constitution and co-wrote The Federalist Papers to promote its ratification.
- Doctors often called James Madison frail and recommended programs to improve his strength and stamina, including a stay at Warm Springs spa in Virginia.
- He was married to Dolley Madison, who was known for her grace and charm as First Lady, and for saving important documents and a portrait of George Washington during the burning of the White House by the British in 1814.
- James Madison is the only U.S. president to have ever led troops into battle while serving as president. During the War of 1812, he rode out to the front lines to observe the fighting and rallied the troops during the Battle of Bladensburg.
- Madison was very shy and introverted. He struggled with public speaking.

Ja mes Monroe

NICKNAME: "The Last Founding Father," "The Era of Good Feelings President," and "The Last Cocked Hat"
BORN: April 28, 1758, in Westmoreland County, Virginia
POLITICAL PARTY: Democratic-Republican
TERM OF OFFICE: March 4, 1817 – March 3, 1825
VICE PRESIDENT: Daniel D. Tompkins
AGE AT INAUGURATION: 58 years
NUMBER OF TERMS: Two full terms
PARENTS:
Spence Monroe
Elizabeth Jones Monroe
MARRIED: Elizabeth "Eliza" Kortright Monroe (1768-1830), on February 16, 1786
CHILDREN: Elizabeth, James, Maria
PETS: a spaniel
EDUCATION: Graduated from College of William and Mary (1776)
RELIGION: Episcopalian
OCCUPATION: Lawyer, public official
OTHER GOVERNMENT POSITIONS: Member of Continental Congress, 1783-86; U.S. Senator, 1790-94; Minister to France, 1794-96; Governor of Virginia, 1799-1802; Minister to France and England, 1803-07; Secretary of State, 1811-17 (under Madison); Secretary of War, 1814-15 (under Madison)
MILITARY SERVICE: Major, Continental Army (1775-1777); Colonel, Virginia Militia (1777-1780)
PRESIDENTIAL SALARY: $25,000/year
DIED: July 4, 1831, in New York, New York
AGE AT DEATH: 73 years
CAUSE OF DEATH: Tuberculosis
BURIED: Richmond, Virginia

James Monroe

5th President of the United States (1817 – 1825)

James Monroe was born in Westmoreland County, Virginia, and grew up on his family's plantation. As a child, he received a classical education and showed a keen interest in books and learning.

Monroe's political career began during the American Revolution when he served in the Continental Army. He was wounded at the Battle of Trenton and later served as an aide to then Governor of Virginia, Thomas Jefferson. After the war, Monroe studied law under Thomas Jefferson and became a practicing attorney in Virginia.

During his presidency, Monroe oversaw a period of American expansion and nationalism. He signed the Missouri Compromise, which maintained the balance of power between free and slave states in the Union.

Monroe also oversaw the acquisition of the Louisiana Territory from France and the establishment of the Monroe Doctrine, which declared that the United States would not tolerate European interference in the affairs of the Western Hemisphere.

After his presidency, Monroe continued to be active in public life. He served as governor of Virginia and later as a U.S. Senator. He was a supporter of the American Colonization Society, which aimed to resettle freed slaves in Africa.

Besides his political accomplishments, Monroe was also known for his personal integrity and humility. He was widely respected for his honesty and his dedication to public service.

Fun Facts:

- Monroe was the last of the Founding Fathers to serve as president. He was also the third president to die on Independence Day, July 4th, after Thomas Jefferson and John Adams.
- Monroe was wounded during the Battle of Trenton in the American Revolution. He was hit in the left shoulder by a musket ball which caused severe bleeding by severing an artery. He was then carried away from the battle site while bleeding profusely. Doctor John Riker intervened by clamping the artery, saving Monroe from bleeding to death.
- Paul Jennings, a slave who served as a footman and later a valet to President Madison, portrayed Madison as a frugal and temperate individual who possessed only a single suit, associated with Thomas Jefferson, and was so cautious with alcohol that he likely never consumed "a quart of brandy in his whole life."
- In 1794, President George Washington chose Monroe as Ambassador to France. Things got worse when the controversial Jay's Treaty was signed in November 1794. Washington let Monroe go from his job in 1796 because Monroe did not like the treaty.
- He initially did not like the Constitution. Monroe refused to go to a meeting where the Constitution was written in 1787 and voiced his opposition at Virginia's ratification meeting. He later changed his mind and supported it after he asked for a strong bill of rights.
- He was the last president of the "Virginia Dynasty." The other presidents of the Virginia Dynasty were George Washington, Thomas Jefferson, James Madison, and James Monroe.

CHAPTER 2

ERA OF THE COMMON MAN (1828–1854)

The Era of the Common Man, also known as the Jacksonian Era, spanned from 1828 to 1854 and was characterized by a focus on democracy and populism in American politics. The era is named after Andrew Jackson, the seventh President of the United States, who was a symbol of the common man and his values. The following is a detailed chronology of the major events that occurred during this time period:

1828:

- Andrew Jackson elected as the seventh President of the United States, defeating incumbent John Quincy Adams in a contentious and divisive election.
- Congress passes The Tariff of Abominations, which raises tariffs on imported goods to protect American industry but angers southern states who rely on foreign trade.

1829:

- Jackson inaugurated as president, and his supporters hold a raucous celebration at the White House that becomes known as the "Inaugural Brawl."
- Jackson begins his policy of "rotation in office," which involves replacing government officials with his own supporters and allies.

1830:

- The Maysville Road veto occurs, where Jackson vetoes a bill to provide federal funding for a road in Kentucky, arguing that it is a state issue.
- Indian Removal Act signed into law, which allows the forced removal of Native American tribes from their ancestral lands in the southeastern United States and their relocation to Indian Territory (present-day Oklahoma).
- The Indian Removal Act begins to be enforced, leading to the forced relocation of thousands of Native Americans, including the Cherokee on the Trail of Tears.

1831:

- Nat Turner's slave rebellion occurs in Virginia, leading to a crackdown on abolitionist activity in the South.

1832:

- The Bank War occurs, where Jackson vetoes the recharter of the Second Bank of the United States, which he views as a tool of the wealthy elite.
- South Carolina passes the Ordinance of Nullification, which declares federal tariffs unconstitutional and threatens to secede from the Union.

1833:

- The Compromise Tariff passes, which gradually reduces tariffs over the next decade in response to South Carolina's nullification threat.
- The Force Bill passes, which gave the president the power to use military force to enforce federal law.

1835:

- The Texas Revolution begins, with Texan rebels fighting for independence from Mexico.

1836:

- The Battle of the Alamo occurs, where a group of Texans, including Davy Crockett and Jim Bowie, are killed by Mexican forces.

- Texas declares its independence from Mexico, and Sam Houston becomes the first president of the Republic of Texas.

1837:

- Martin Van Buren inaugurated as the Eighth President of the United States, inheriting a financial crisis and an economic depression.

1840:

- William Henry Harrison elected as the ninth President of the United States, running on a populist platform and using the slogan "Tippecanoe and Tyler Too."
- Harrison dies just one month into his presidency, making him the shortest-serving president in U.S. history.

1841:

- John Tyler becomes the tenth President of the United States after Harrison's death, but he quickly falls out of favor with his own party and faces opposition from both Democrats and Whigs.

1845:

- Texas annexed into the United States, becoming the 28th state.

1850:

- The Compromise of 1850 passes, which resolves several disputes related to slavery and territorial expansion.
- The Fugitive Slave Act passes as part of the compromise, which requires the return of escaped slaves to their owners and causes controversy in the North.

1854:

- The Kansas-Nebraska Act passes, which allows for popular sovereignty (voting by residents) to determine whether slavery will be allowed in the territories of Kansas.

John Quincy Adams

6th President of the United States (1825 – 1829)

John Quincy Adams

NICKNAME: "Old Man Eloquent," "The Hell-Hound of Abolition," "The Massachusetts Madman," "The President Who Would Not Fight, "The Accidental President," and "JQA"
BORN: July 11, 1767, in Braintree (now Quincy), Massachusetts
POLITICAL PARTY: Democratic-Republican and National Republican
TERM OF OFFICE: March 4, 1825 – March 3, 1829
VICE PRESIDENT: John C. Calhoun
AGE AT INAUGURATION: 57 years
NUMBER OF TERMS: One full term
PARENTS:
John Adams
Abigail Smith Adams
MARRIED: Louisa Catherine Johnson Adams (1775-1852), on July 26, 1797
CHILDREN: George, John II, Charles, Louisa, an unnamed son.
PETS: an alligator; silkworms
EDUCATION: Graduated from Harvard College (1787)
RELIGION: Unitarian
OCCUPATION: Lawyer, public official
OTHER GOVERNMENT POSITIONS: Secretary to U.S. Minister to Russia, 1781; Minister to the Netherlands, 1794; Minister to Prussia, 1797-1801; U.S. Senator, 1803-08; Minister to Russia, 1809-11; Peace Commissioner at Treaty of Ghent, 1814; Secretary of State, 1817-25 (under Monroe); Member of U.S. House of Representatives, 1831-48
MILITARY SERVICE: None
PRESIDENTIAL SALARY: $25,000/year
DIED: February 23, 1848, in Washington, D.C.
AGE AT DEATH: 80 years
CAUSE OF DEATH: Stroke
BURIED: Quincy, Massachusetts

John Quincy Adams was the son of former U.S. President John Adams and Abigail Adams. He had a privileged childhood, growing up in a family of prominent politicians and intellectuals. His father played an instrumental role in the American Revolution and later served as the second President of the United States. John Quincy followed his father's example by pursuing a career in politics, as his father raised him with a strong sense of duty and a commitment to public service.

As a young man, Adams served as a diplomat in Europe and played a key role in negotiating the Treaty of Ghent, which ended the War of 1812 between the United States and Britain. He also served as a U.S. Senator from Massachusetts and as Secretary of State under President James Monroe. During his tenure as Secretary of State, Adams helped to formulate the Monroe Doctrine, which declared that the United States would not tolerate European interference in the affairs of the Western Hemisphere.

In 1824, Adams ran for President of the United States and won a contentious election against Andrew Jackson. During his presidency, Adams pursued an ambitious agenda of national improvement, including the construction of roads, canals, and other infrastructure projects. He also advocated to expand education and scientific research and supported the establishment of a national university.

One of Adams' most significant accomplishments during his presidency was his successful negotiation of the Adams-Onís Treaty with Spain, which secured U.S. control over Florida and established the western boundary of the United States. He also worked to improve relations with Native American tribes and signed several treaties with them that recognized their sovereignty and established boundaries between their territories and those of the United States.

After leaving office, Adams continued to serve in public life, serving as a U.S. Representative from Massachusetts until his death. He was a staunch opponent of slavery and played an important role in the abolitionist movement, including successfully arguing before the U.S. Supreme Court on behalf of a group of Africans who had mutinied aboard a slave ship and were being held as property. Adams' dedication to public service and his commitment to principles of justice and equality continue to be remembered and celebrated today.

Fun Facts:

- Adams was the first president whose father was also a president, John Adams.
- He kept a pet alligator gifted by Marquis de Lafayette at the White House.
- After leaving the presidency, Adams served in the House of Representatives for 17 years, becoming one of the most prominent and vocal opponents of slavery in Congress.
- His support was important in Congress' decision to establish the Smithsonian Institution in 1846.
- Adams had a unique approach to exercise. He would often take long walks, take breaks during his workday to do calisthenics, and frequently went skinny dipping in the Potomac River.
- He was a prolific writer - Adams wrote in his diary nearly every day from the age of 12 until his death at 80, totaling over 14,000 pages.

Andrew Jackson (signature)

NICKNAME: "Old Hickory," "Sharp Knife," and "Indian Killer"
BORN: March 15, 1767, in the Waxhaw area, on North Carolina-South Carolina border
POLITICAL PARTY: Democratic
TERM OF OFFICE: March 4, 1829 – March 3, 1837
VICE PRESIDENT: John C. Calhoun 1825-1832), Martin Van Buren (1833–1837)
AGE AT INAUGURATION: 61 years
NUMBER OF TERMS: Two full terms
PARENTS:
Andrew Jackson
Elizabeth Hutchinson Jackson
MARRIED: Rachel Donelson Jackson (1767-1828), in August 1791 and in a second ceremony on January 17, 1794
CHILDREN: Adopted children Andrew Jr. and Lyncoya
PETS: horses named Truxton, Sam Patches, Emily, Lady Nashville, and Bolivia; Poll the parrot; ponies
EDUCATION: No formal education
RELIGION: Presbyterian
OCCUPATION: Lawyer, soldier, public official
OTHER GOVERNMENT POSITIONS: Member of U.S. House of Representatives, 1796-97; United States Senator, 1797-98; Justice on Tennessee Supreme Court, 1798-1804; Governor of the Florida Territory, 1821; U.S. Senator, 1823-25
MILITARY SERVICE: Captain, Davidson County Militia (1792-1802); Major General, Tennessee Militia (1802-1814); Major General, U.S. Army (1814-1821)
PRESIDENTIAL SALARY: $25,000/year
DIED: June 8, 1845, at the Hermitage in Nashville, Tennessee
AGE AT DEATH: 78 years
CAUSE OF DEATH: Renal Failure
BURIED: Nashville, Tennessee

Andrew Jackson

7th President of the United States (1829 – 1837)

Andrew Jackson was born in the Carolina Waxhaw region to Irish immigrant parents. He grew up in poverty, as his father died before he was born, and his mother died when he was only 14 years old. Jackson was largely self-educated and had a fiery temperament, often getting into fights and trouble as a young man.

Before his presidency, Jackson had a successful military career, becoming a national hero after leading American forces to victory in the Battle of New Orleans during the War of 1812. He also played a crucial role in the First Seminole War, where he led an invasion of Spanish Florida to fight against the Seminole tribe.

During his presidency, Jackson implemented policies that favored the common man and sought to limit the power of the wealthy elite. He signed the Indian Removal Act, which forced Native American tribes to move from their ancestral lands in the southeastern United States to reservations in Oklahoma. This policy, known as the Trail of Tears, resulted in the deaths of thousands of Native Americans.

Jackson also vetoed the re-chartering of the Second Bank of the United States, which he believed was corrupt and only benefited the wealthy elite. This move led to a financial crisis and contributed to the Panic of 1837.

After his presidency, Jackson retired to his home in Tennessee, known as the Hermitage. He remained active in politics and continued to be a vocal advocate for the common man until his death. Jackson also served as a mentor to James K. Polk, who later became the 11th President of the United States.

Overall, Andrew Jackson is remembered as a controversial figure in American history, with some admiring him for his military victories and populist policies, while others criticize him for his treatment of Native Americans and his handling of the national economy.

Fun Facts:

- Jackson was involved in many duels throughout his life, and he reportedly killed at least one person in a duel. In one famous duel, he was shot in the chest but still killed his opponent.
- He had a pet parrot named Poll that he taught to swear. The bird was known for cursing and screaming obscenities in the White House, and it had to be removed from Jackson's funeral because of its foul language.
- He has appeared on the $20 bill since the series of 1928. The placement of Jackson on the $20 bill is surprising; as president, he vehemently opposed both the National Bank and use of paper money.
- Jackson was a staunch defender of the Union and threatened to use military force to prevent any state from seceding. We often credit him with preventing the secession of South Carolina in the early 1830s.
- He was the first president to have an assassination attempt made against him while in office. A man named Richard Lawrence attempted to shoot Jackson with two pistols, but both misfired. Jackson beat Lawrence with his cane until other members of the crowd stopped him.
- Jackson's nickname was "Old Hickory" because of his toughness and endurance during the War of 1812.
- In 1833, Jackson became the first president to ride a train.

Martin Van Buren

8th President of the United States (1837 – 1841)

M. Van Buren

NICKNAME: "Old Kinderhook," "The Red Fox," "The Little Magician," "Martin Van Ruin," "The Careful Dutchman," "The Aristocrat", The Prince of Albany," "The American Talleyrand," "The Enchanter," "The Great Manager," "The Master Spirit," and "The Mistletoe Politician"
BORN: December 5, 1782, in Kinderhook, New York
POLITICAL PARTY: Democratic
TERM OF OFFICE: March 4, 1837 – March 3, 1841
VICE PRESIDENT: Richard M. Johnson
AGE AT INAUGURATION: 54 years
NUMBER OF TERMS: One full term
PARENTS:
Abraham Van Buren
Maria Hoes Van Buren
MARRIED: Hannah Hoes Van Buren (1783-1819), on February 21, 1807
CHILDREN: Abraham, John, Martin Jr., Winfield, Smith, and an unnamed daughter.
PETS: two tiger cubs
EDUCATION: Graduated from Kinderhook Academy (1796)
RELIGION: Dutch Reformed
OCCUPATION: Lawyer, public official
OTHER GOVERNMENT POSITIONS: New York State Senator, 1813-15; New York Attorney-General, 1815-19; U.S. Senator, 1821-29; Governor of New York, 1829; Secretary of State, 1829-1831 (under Jackson); Minister to England, 1831; Vice President, 1833-1837 (under Jackson)
MILITARY SERVICE: None
PRESIDENTIAL SALARY: $25,000/year
DIED: July 24, 1862, in Kinderhook, New York
AGE AT DEATH: 79 years
CAUSE OF DEATH: Asthma
BURIED: Kinderhook, New York

Martin Van Buren was born in Kinderhook, New York, and grew up in a Dutch-speaking household. His father was a tavern owner and farmer, and his mother was from a prominent Dutch family. Van Buren received a limited formal education, but he was an avid reader and taught himself law.

Before becoming president, Van Buren served as the governor of New York, a U.S. senator, and the secretary of state under President Andrew Jackson. He played a pivotal role in the establishment of the Democratic Party and the development of a formidable political apparatus to support Jackson's presidency.

As president, Van Buren faced several challenges, including a financial crisis known as the Panic of 1837. He implemented policies to try to stabilize the economy, including creating an independent treasury system to separate government funds from private banks.

Van Buren was also a powerful advocate for limited government and states' rights. He opposed the expansion of slavery into new territories, but he did not support abolitionism.

After leaving office, Van Buren remained active in politics and served as a vocal opponent of slavery and an advocate for free trade. He played a role in the organization of the Free Soil Party, a political group that stood against the spread of slavery into new territories.

Besides his political accomplishments, Van Buren was known for his stylish dress and his charm and wit. During the early 19th century, he exerted a significant influence on the political scene of the United States, thanks to his adept political skills, shrewd negotiation tactics, and pivotal role in shaping the country's political landscape.

Fun Facts:

- Martin Van Buren was the first president of the United States who was born a United States citizen, rather than a British subject. He was born in Kinderhook, New York, on December 5, 1782.
- Van Buren was only about 5'6" tall, which made him one of the shortest presidents in U.S. history.
- His nickname was the "Little Magician" because of his small stature and his skill in political maneuvering.
- He was the first president to be born after the signing of the Declaration of Independence.
- Van Buren was the first president to be born a native speaker of a language other than English. His first language was Dutch.
- He was the first president to be born after the American Revolution.
- Van Buren was the first president to have been a widower at the time of his inauguration. His wife, Hannah, had died in 1819.
- He was the first president to use the term "OK" in a presidential message. The term originated from his nickname, "Old Kinderhook," which was abbreviated as "O.K."
- He was the first president to have been born in a house that was built after the American Revolution.
- Van Buren's favorite hobby was playing cards.

William Henry Harrison (signature)

NICKNAME: "Old Tippecanoe," "Old Tip," "General Mum," and "Farmer President"
BORN: February 9, 1773, in Berkeley, Virginia
POLITICAL PARTY: Whig
TERM OF OFFICE: March 4, 1841 – April 4, 1841
VICE PRESIDENT: John Tyler
AGE AT INAUGURATION: 68 years
NUMBER OF TERMS: Died 31 days into term
PARENTS:
Benjamin Harrison
Elizabeth Bassett Harrison
MARRIED: Anna Tuthill Symmes Harrison (1775-1864), on November 25, 1795
CHILDREN: With Anna Tuthill Symmes Harrison: Elizabeth, John, Lucy, William Jr., John, Benjamin, Mary, Carter, Anna, James; Alleged children with Dilcia (one of his slaves): Marie and five other children
PETS: a goat named Billy and a Durham cow named Sukey
EDUCATION: Attended Hampden-Sydney College
RELIGION: Episcopalian
OCCUPATION: Soldier, public official
OTHER GOVERNMENT POSITIONS: Secretary of Northwest Territory, 1798; Territorial Delegate to Congress, 1799-1801; Territorial Governor of Indiana, 1801-13; U.S. Congressman from Ohio, 1816-19; U.S. Senator, 1825-28; Minister to Colombia, 1828-29
MILITARY SERVICE: Captain, U.S. Army (1791-1798); Major General, U.S. Army, (1812-1814)
PRESIDENTIAL SALARY: $25,000/year
DIED: April 4, 1841, in Washington, D.C.
AGE AT DEATH: 68 years
CAUSE OF DEATH: Pneumonia
BURIED: North Bend, Ohio

William Henry Harrison

9th President of the United States (1841)

William Henry Harrison was born into a prominent Virginia family and had a comfortable childhood with access to a good education. He later joined the army and served as a junior officer in battles against Native American tribes in the Northwest Territory.

During his presidency, which lasted only 32 days, Harrison made some notable accomplishments. He gave a lengthy inaugural address on a cold and wet day without wearing a coat, which unfortunately led to him catching a cold and dying shortly thereafter. Nevertheless, he lay the groundwork for future economic growth by advocating to expand the nation's infrastructure, particularly its transportation system. He also sought to strengthen the federal government's power over the states, advocating for a stronger executive branch and a more assertive federal judiciary.

After his brief presidency, Harrison's legacy continued. His grandson, Benjamin Harrison, would later become the 23rd President of the United States. Additionally, William Henry Harrison's image and military record were used to help popularize the Whig Party, which saw itself as the heir to the Federalist Party and emphasized strong national unity and economic development.

Overall, William Henry Harrison's legacy was one of military service and political ambition. Despite his short tenure in office, he left a lasting impact on the country, particularly to advocate for economic growth and a stronger federal government.

Fun Facts:

- William Henry Harrison served for only 32 days in 1841, making him the shortest-serving U.S. President in history.
- He was the first U.S. President to die in office, and his death sparked a constitutional crisis over the line of succession.
- He was famous for his long and rambling speeches, which often lasted for hours. His inaugural address, delivered on a cold and rainy day, lasted for over two hours and he refused to wear a coat or hat.
- Harrison was the last U.S. President to be born a British subject, as he was born in Virginia in 1773, before the American Revolution.
- He was also the last U.S. President to own slaves while in office, and he brought several enslaved people with him to the White House.
- He was a military hero who served in the War of 1812 and defeated the Native American confederacy led by Tecumseh at the Battle of Tippecanoe.
- He was also known for his unconventional medical treatments, including bleeding and purging, which likely contributed to his death from pneumonia just one month after taking office.
- Harrison's campaign slogan was "Tippecanoe and Tyler Too," which referred to his victory at the Battle of Tippecanoe and his running mate, John Tyler.
- He was the first sitting U.S. President to have his photograph taken, although it has been since lost to history.
- Harrison's father, Benjamin Harrison V, was one of the signers of the Declaration of Independence.

John Tyler (signature)

NICKNAME: "Accidental President"
BORN: March 29, 1790, in Greenway, Virginia
POLITICAL PARTY: Whig and Unaffiliated
TERM OF OFFICE: April 6, 1841 – March 3, 1845
VICE PRESIDENT: None
AGE AT INAUGURATION: 51 years
NUMBER OF TERMS: One partial term (3 years and 11 months)
PARENTS:
John Tyler
Mary Marot Armistead Tyler
MARRIED: Letitia Chrisitan Tyler (1790-1842), on March 29, 1813; Julia Gardiner Tyler (1820-1889), on June 26, 1844
CHILDREN: With Letitia Christian: Mary, Robert, John, Letitia, Elizabeth, Anne Contesse, Alice, Tazewell; With Julia Gardiner: David, John, Julia, Lachlan, Lyon, Robert Fitzwalter, Pearl
PETS: a greyhound and a horse
EDUCATION: Graduated from the College of William and Mary (1807)
RELIGION: Episcopalian
OCCUPATION: Lawyer
OTHER GOVERNMENT POSITIONS: Member of Virginia House of Delegates, 1811-16; Member of U.S. House of Representatives, 1816-21; Virginia State Legislator, 1823-25; Governor of Virginia, 1825-26; U.S. Senator, 1827-36; Vice President, 1841 (under W. H. Harrison); Member of Confederate States Congress, 1861-62
MILITARY SERVICE: Captain, Charles City Rifles (Virginia militia company) (1813)
PRESIDENTIAL SALARY: $25,000/year
DIED: January 18, 1862, in Richmond, Virginia
AGE AT DEATH: 71 years
CAUSE OF DEATH: Stroke
BURIED: Richmond, Virginia

John Tyler

10th President of the United States (1841 – 1845)

John Tyler was born into a prominent Virginia family and had a privileged childhood. He attended the College of William and Mary and studied law, but his father's death forced him to leave school and take over the family plantation.

Before his presidency, Tyler had a successful career in politics. He served in the Virginia House of Delegates, the U.S. House of Representatives, and the U.S. Senate.

During his presidency, Tyler faced significant challenges, including tensions with Great Britain and a financial crisis that led to the collapse of several banks. He was also responsible for overseeing the annexation of Texas, which was a controversial and divisive issue.

One of Tyler's notable accomplishments during his presidency was the signing of the Webster-Ashburton Treaty in 1842. This treaty established the northeastern border between the United States and Canada and helped to improve relations between the two countries.

After his presidency, Tyler remained active in politics and was a vocal advocate for states' rights and the Confederacy during the Civil War. He was even elected to the Confederate Congress, making him the only former U.S. president to serve in the government of another country.

Besides his political career, Tyler was a successful businessman and owned several plantations throughout his life. He was also a prolific writer and authored many books and articles on politics and history.

Overall, John Tyler was a significant figure in American politics and played a role in many important events throughout his life, including his presidency, the annexation of Texas, and the Civil War.

Fun Facts:

- John Tyler was the first vice president to become president because of the death of a sitting president. He assumed the presidency after William Henry Harrison died just 32 days into his term.
- He was the only president to be expelled from his own political party while in office. This was because he opposed the Whig Party's agenda and vetoed several of their bills.
- He was also the only president to serve in both the Confederate Congress and the U.S. Congress. He was elected to the Confederate Congress after his home state of Virginia seceded from the Union during the Civil War.
- Tyler had 15 children, the most of any American president. His last child was born when he was 70 years old, and one of his grandsons is still alive today.
- He was the first president to have a veto overridden by Congress. This happened in 1845, when he vetoed a bill to reestablish the Bank of the United States.
- Tyler married his second wife, Julia Gardiner, when he was 54 and she was 22. Their wedding was controversial and caused a scandal in Washington, D.C.
- He was a big fan of music and enjoyed playing the violin. He would often play for guests at the White House.

Jamez K Polk

NICKNAME: "Young Hickory," "Napoleon of the Stump," "Polk the Purposeful," and "Dark Horse President"
BORN: November 2, 1795, in Mecklenburg County, North Carolina
POLITICAL PARTY: Democratic
TERM OF OFFICE: March 4, 1845 – March 4, 1849
VICE PRESIDENT: George M. Dallas
AGE AT INAUGURATION: 49 years
NUMBER OF TERMS: One full term
PARENTS:
Samuel Polk
Jane Knox Polk
MARRIED: Sarah Childress Polk (1803-1891), on January 1, 1824
CHILDREN: None
PETS: None
EDUCATION: Graduated from the University of North Carolina (1818)
RELIGION: Presbyterian
OCCUPATION: Lawyer, public official
OTHER GOVERNMENT POSITIONS: Member of Tennessee House of Representatives, 1823-25;Member of U.S. House of Representatives, 1825-39; Speaker of the House, 1835-39; Governor of Tennessee, 1839-41
MILITARY SERVICE: Colonel, Tennessee Militia (1821)
PRESIDENTIAL SALARY: $25,000/year
DIED: June 15, 1849, in Nashville, Tennessee
AGE AT DEATH: 53 years
CAUSE OF DEATH: Cholera
BURIED: Nashville, Tennessee

James K. Polk

11th President of the United States (1845 – 1849)

James K. Polk was born in Mecklenburg County, North Carolina, to a family of farmers. His family moved to Tennessee when he was a child, where he grew up on a farm and received a basic education. As a young man, Polk studied law and became a lawyer, eventually serving as a member of the Tennessee state legislature and as a member of the U.S. House of Representatives.

During his presidency, Polk is perhaps best known for his expansionist policies, which saw the U.S. gain a significant amount of territory, including California, Texas, and much of the Southwest. He also oversaw the construction of the Smithsonian Institution, the establishment of the U.S. Naval Academy, and the signing of the Treaty of Guadalupe Hidalgo, which ended the Mexican-American War.

After his presidency, Polk retired from politics and returned to his home in Tennessee. He remained active in public life, however, serving as a trustee of the University of North Carolina and working to promote the development of railroads and other infrastructure in the South.

Besides his political accomplishments, Polk is also remembered for his strong work ethic and his commitment to public service. He was known for his attention to detail and his ability to work tirelessly to achieve his goals, and he remains one of the most successful and effective presidents in American history.

Fun Facts:

- People referred to James K. Polk as the "dark horse" candidate because he was relatively unknown prior to winning the Democratic nomination for President in 1844.
- During his presidency, Polk oversaw the annexation of Texas, the Oregon Treaty, and the Mexican-American War, which resulted in the acquisition of California, New Mexico, Arizona, Nevada, Utah, and parts of Colorado, Wyoming, Kansas, and Oklahoma.
- He was known for being a workaholic, often working 12-14 hours a day, and he achieved all of his campaign promises in his single term as President.
- Polk was the youngest person to be Speaker of the House of Representatives, a position he held before becoming President.
- James K. Polk and his wife Sarah Childress Polk did not have any children, but they raised a nephew, Marshall Tate Polk. Marshall Tate Polk, Jr. was the son of President Polk's brother, Marshall Tate Polk, who died one month before the child's birth.
- He is the only president to have served as Speaker of the House of Representatives and as governor of a state (Tennessee) before becoming president.
- He was the youngest person ever elected to the presidency at the time of his inauguration, at 49.
- Polk promised to serve only one term as president and kept his promise, dying just three months after leaving office.
- Polk is buried on the grounds of the Tennessee State Capitol in Nashville, making him the only president buried on state property.

Zachary Taylor (signature)

NICKNAME: "Old Rough and Ready," "Hero of Buena Vista," "Old Zack," "Major General Taylor," and "The Louisiana Patriot"
BORN: November 24, 1784, near Barboursville, Virginia
POLITICAL PARTY: Whig
TERM OF OFFICE: March 5, 1849 – July 9, 1850
VICE PRESIDENT: Millard Fillmore
AGE AT INAUGURATION: 64 years
NUMBER OF TERMS: Died 1 year, 4 months, and 5 days into term
PARENTS:
Lieutenant Colonel Richard Taylor
Sarah Dabney Strother Taylor
MARRIED: Margaret Mackall Smith Taylor (1788-1852), on June 21, 1810
CHILDREN: Ann, Sarah, Octavia, Margaret, Mary, Richard
PETS: Old Whitey (Taylor's warhorse) and Apollo (formerly a "trick pony" from a circus, a present for Taylor's daughter Betty and resided in the White House stables with Old Whitey)
EDUCATION: No formal education
RELIGION: Episcopalian
OCCUPATION: Soldier
OTHER GOVERNMENT POSITIONS: None
MILITARY SERVICE: Major General, U.S. Army (1805-1815, 1816-1849)
PRESIDENTIAL SALARY: $25,000/year
DIED: July 9, 1850, in Washington, D.C.
AGE AT DEATH: 65 years
CAUSE OF DEATH: Stomach Virus (a death by poisoning theory was disproved in 2014)
BURIED: Louisville, Kentucky

Zachary Taylor

12th President of the United States (1849 – 1850)

Zachary Taylor was born into a wealthy family in Virginia. He grew up in Kentucky and received a limited formal education, but he was known for his strength and athleticism, and he enjoyed hunting and fishing.

Before becoming president, Taylor had a long and distinguished military career. He served in the War of 1812, the Black Hawk War, and the Second Seminole War. He became a national hero for his victories in the Mexican-American War, including the battles of Palo Alto and Buena Vista.

As president, Taylor had a mixed record. He opposed the expansion of slavery into the western territories, which put him at odds with many southern politicians. He also opposed the Compromise of 1850, which would have admitted California as a free state and strengthened the Fugitive Slave Act. However, Taylor could not accomplish much during his brief presidency, as he died after only 16 months in office.

Taylor's cause of death is not entirely clear, but it is believed that he contracted a gastrointestinal illness, possibly from eating contaminated food or drinking contaminated water. His vice president, Millard Fillmore, succeeded him as president and supported the Compromise of 1850 that Taylor had opposed.

Fun Facts:

- Taylor, who owned over 150 slaves on plantations in Kentucky, Mississippi, and Louisiana, was the last U.S. President to own slaves while in office. Although slavery was legal at the time, his ownership of slaves was a controversial issue during his presidency.
- Taylor was not a politician before he became president. He had no experience in politics or government, but he was a successful military general who had won several key battles in the Mexican-American War.
- He was known as "Old Rough and Ready" due to his rugged appearance and the rough clothing he wore while on military campaigns.
- Taylor was not a particularly well-educated man. He had only about a year of formal schooling, and was largely self-taught.
- He was a heavy smoker and would smoke cigars during military campaigns.
- Taylor's presidency was one of the shortest in American history, lasting only 16 months before his death. There were rumors of poisoning, but these were never substantiated. Inconclusive tests followed his exhumation in 1991, while a 2014 exhumation confirmed he was not poisoned.
- His daughter, Sarah Knox Taylor, married future Confederate president Jefferson Davis.
- His portrait appears on the $10,000 bill, which was last printed in 1945 and is no longer in circulation.
- He delayed his inauguration by a day because he refused to swear the oath of office on a Sunday.
- Taylor was the second president to die in office, after William Henry Harrison.
- He was related to another American president, James Madison, and two of his other ancestors who came over on the Mayflower were Isaac Allerton and Fear Brewster.

Millard Fillmore (signature)

NICKNAME: "The American Louis Philippe," "The Accidental President," "The Compromise President," and "The Last Whig President"
BORN: January 7, 1800, in Locke Township (now Summerhill), New York
POLITICAL PARTY: Whig
TERM OF OFFICE: July 9, 1850 – March 3, 1853
VICE PRESIDENT: None
AGE AT INAUGURATION: 50 years
NUMBER OF TERMS: One partial term (2 years, 7 months, and 23 days)
PARENTS:
Nathaniel Fillmore
Phoebe Millard Fillmore
Eunice Love (Stepmother)
MARRIED: Eunice Love Married: Abigail Powers Fillmore (1798-1853), on February 5, 1826; Caroline Carmichael McIntosh (1813-1881), on February 10, 1858
CHILDREN: Millard, Mary
PETS: None
EDUCATION: No formal education
RELIGION: Unitarian
OCCUPATION: Lawyer, public official
OTHER GOVERNMENT POSITIONS: Member of New York State Assembly, 1828-31; Member of U.S. House of Representatives, 1833-35 and 1837-45; Comptroller of New York, 1847; Vice President, 1849-1850 (under Taylor)
MILITARY SERVICE: Major, New York Militia (1820s-1830s); Captain, New York Guard (1860s-1870s)
PRESIDENTIAL SALARY: $25,000/year
DIED: March 8, 1874 in Buffalo, New York
AGE AT DEATH: 74 years
CAUSE OF DEATH: Stroke
BURIED: Buffalo, New York

Millard Fillmore

13th President of the United States (1850 – 1853)

Millard Fillmore was born into a poor family in upstate New York. His father was a farmer and small business owner, and Fillmore worked on the family farm from a young age. Despite his humble beginnings, Fillmore was a talented student and showed an early aptitude for law.

The people elected Fillmore to the New York State Assembly in 1829 after he quickly made a name for himself as a young lawyer. During his time in the Assembly, Fillmore became known for his support of education reform and his advocacy for the abolition of the death penalty.

Fillmore's most notable accomplishments during his presidency include his support for the Compromise of 1850, which helped to ease tensions between the North and South over the issue of slavery. As part of the Compromise, Fillmore signed into law the Fugitive Slave Act, which required the return of runaway slaves to their owners. While this decision was controversial and unpopular in the North, it was seen as a necessary step to avoid the outbreak of civil war.

After leaving office, Fillmore continued to be an active public figure and was involved in several philanthropic and civic organizations. He helped to establish the University of Buffalo and served as its first chancellor. Fillmore was also a founding member of the Buffalo Historical Society and worked to preserve and promote the city's history.

Throughout his life, Millard Fillmore was known for his integrity, his dedication to public service, and his commitment to education and civic engagement. Despite facing criticism and controversy during his presidency, he remained committed to doing what he believed was best for the country and worked tirelessly to promote unity and progress.

Fun Facts:

- Fillmore was the first U.S. President to have a bathtub installed in the White House. Before this, presidents had to use portable tubs.
- Fillmore was the first president to have a stepmother, as his father remarried after his mother's death.
- He was the first president to send a diplomat to Japan, helping to establish trade relations between the two countries.
- Fillmore established the White House Library during his presidency, which helped to expand the collection of books available to the president and his family.
- His last words were reportedly, "The nourishment is palatable."
- Fillmore married his former teacher, Abigail Powers, who was 10 years younger than him and had been his teacher when he was a student.
- He helped found the University at Buffalo, which was then called the University of Buffalo.
- He was the first president to visit California while in office.
- Fillmore was an advocate for religious tolerance, and he was instrumental in securing the right of Jews to serve in public office.
- He was the first president to ride on a steam-powered train.
- He was the last U.S. President to not have a formal inauguration ceremony.
- He was the only president who never had a vice president.

CHAPTER 3

CIVIL WAR AND RECONSTRUCTION ERA (1854–1896)

The Civil War and Reconstruction Era (1854-1896) was a tumultuous period in United States history characterized by political, social, and economic upheaval. It began with the Kansas-Nebraska Act of 1854 and ended with the Plessy v. Ferguson Supreme Court decision in 1896. Below is a detailed chronology of events during this period:

1854-1860: Antebellum Period

1854 - Kansas-Nebraska Act: Congress passed this act which allowed the territories of Kansas and Nebraska to determine whether they would allow slavery. This led to violence and conflict between pro-slavery and anti-slavery settlers.

1857 - Dred Scott Decision: The Supreme Court ruled that African Americans, whether free or enslaved, were not citizens and had no legal standing to sue for their freedom. This decision further divided the country along pro- and anti-slavery lines.

1860 - Election of Abraham Lincoln: Lincoln, a Republican who opposed the expansion of slavery, won the presidential election, causing seven southern states to secede from the Union and form the Confederate States of America.

1861-1865: Civil War

1861 - Fort Sumter: Confederate forces fired on Fort Sumter, a Union stronghold in South Carolina, marking the beginning of the Civil War.

1862 - Emancipation Proclamation: President Lincoln issued this executive order declaring that all slaves in Confederate-held territories were free, which helped to shift the focus of the war to the issue of slavery.

1863 - Gettysburg Address: Lincoln delivered this famous speech at the dedication of the Gettysburg cemetery, emphasizing the importance of preserving the Union and the equality of all people.

1865 - Appomattox Court House: Confederate General Robert E. Lee surrendered to Union General Ulysses S. Grant at Appomattox Court House in Virginia, effectively ending the Civil War.

1865-1877: Reconstruction Period

1865 - Assassination of Lincoln: President Lincoln assassinated by John Wilkes Booth, which led to Andrew Johnson, a Southern Democrat and former slave owner, becoming president.

1865-1866 - Black Codes: Southern states passed laws restricting the rights and freedoms of newly freed African Americans, which led to increased tension and violence.

1867 - Reconstruction Act: Congress passed this act, which divided the former Confederate states into military districts and required them to ratify the 14th Amendment in order to be readmitted to the Union.

1868 - 14th Amendment: This constitutional amendment granted citizenship to all people born or naturalized in the United States, including former slaves, and guaranteed equal protection under the law.

1870 - 15th Amendment: This constitutional amendment prohibited states from denying the right to vote based on race, color, or previous condition of servitude.

1877-1896: Jim Crow Era

1877 - Compromise of 1877: Democrats agreed to support Republican Rutherford B. Hayes in the presidential election in exchange for the withdrawal of federal troops from the South, effectively ending Reconstruction.

1883 - Civil Rights Cases: The Supreme Court ruled Congress could not prohibit discrimination by private individuals or businesses, which weakened the enforcement of civil rights laws.

1890 - Plessy v. Ferguson: The Supreme Court upheld the constitutionality of "separate but equal" facilities for African Americans, which further entrenched segregation in the South.

1896 - Election of William McKinley: McKinley, a Republican who supported high tariffs and industrialization, won the presidential election, marking the end of the Reconstruction Era and the beginning of the Gilded Age.

Franklin Pierce (signature)

NICKNAME: "Young Hickory of the Granite Hills," "The Fainting General," "Fainting Frank," "Handsome Frank," "The Hero of Many a Well-Fought Bottle," and "The Doughface President"
BORN: November 23, 1804, in Hillsborough (now Hillsboro), New Hampshire
POLITICAL PARTY: Democratic
TERM OF OFFICE: March 4, 1853 – March 3, 1857
VICE PRESIDENT: William R. King
AGE AT INAUGURATION: 48 years
NUMBER OF TERMS: One full term
PARENTS:
General Benjamin Pierce
Ann Kendrick Pierce
MARRIED: Jane Means Appleton Pierce (1806-1863), on November 10, 1834
CHILDREN: Franklin Jr., Franklin Robert, Benjamin
PETS: seven tea cup-sized dogs and two birds (all gifts from Japan)
EDUCATION: Graduated from Bowdoin College (1824)
RELIGION: Episcopalian
OCCUPATION: Lawyer, public official
OTHER GOVERNMENT POSITIONS: Served in New Hampshire Legislature, 1829-33; Member of U.S. House of Representatives, 1833-37; U.S. Senate, 1837-42
MILITARY SERVICE: Colonel, New Hampshire Militia (1831-1847); Brigadier General, U.S. Army (1847-1848)
PRESIDENTIAL SALARY: $25,000/year
DIED: October 8, 1869, in Concord, New Hampshire
AGE AT DEATH: 64 years
CAUSE OF DEATH: Cirrhosis of the Liver
BURIED: Concord, New Hampshire

Franklin Pierce

14th President of the United States (1853 – 1857)

Franklin Pierce was raised in New Hampshire and had a difficult childhood marked by personal tragedy. When he was 11 years old, his father died in a freak accident, and Pierce later watched as his own young son died in a train accident before his eyes, which caused him great emotional pain.

Before his presidency, Pierce served in the Mexican-American War, where he displayed bravery and leadership as a brigadier general. He served in Congress and later ran for the Senate and won.

As President, Pierce's most significant accomplishment was his advocacy for the Gadsden Purchase, which added a significant amount of territory to the United States, including parts of modern-day Arizona and New Mexico. However, Pierce's presidency was also marred by controversy and division, particularly around slavery.

After leaving office, Pierce returned to private life and became an advocate for northern unity in the lead-up to the Civil War. He opposed secession and supported the Union cause, even though he disagreed with President Lincoln's policies.

Pierce also worked to improve relations between the United States and Britain, and he played a role in the settlement of a dispute over the San Juan Islands between the two nations.

Throughout his life, Pierce struggled with alcoholism, which likely contributed to his often controversial and divisive political career. Despite this, he remains an interesting figure in American history, both for his accomplishments and his personal struggles.

Fun Facts:

- Pierce was the first and only president from New Hampshire.
- Pierce was known for his love of alcohol and was said to have kept a fully stocked bar in the White House during his presidency.
- He was a Brigadier General in the Mexican-American War, and was wounded at the Battle of Contreras.
- Pierce was a supporter of the expansion of slavery into new territories, and his pro-slavery stance made him unpopular in much of the northern United States.
- Pierce was deeply affected by personal tragedy throughout his life. His first child died shortly after birth, his second child died at the age of four, and his third child died in a train accident while he was president-elect.
- He was the first president to recite his inaugural address from memory, rather than reading from a prepared text.
- He was the only president to keep his entire cabinet for the full four years.
- Pierce was an avid collector of literature and amassed an extensive collection of books throughout his life.
- Pierce was a close friend of Nathaniel Hawthorne, the author of "The Scarlet Letter," and the two men corresponded frequently.
- Pierce's heavy drinking and smoking habits possibly caused him to die of cirrhosis of the liver.
- He is the only president to have affirmed rather than sworn the oath of office at his inauguration.

James Buchanan [signature]

NICKNAME: "Ten-Cent Jimmy," "Bachelor President," and "Old Buck"
BORN: April 23, 1791, in Cove Gap (near Mercersburg), Pennsylvania
POLITICAL PARTY: Democratic
TERM OF OFFICE: March 4, 1857 – March 3, 1861
VICE PRESIDENT: John C. Breckinridge
AGE AT INAUGURATION: 65 years
NUMBER OF TERMS: One full term
PARENTS:
James Buchanan
Elizabeth Speer Buchanan
MARRIED: Never married. The White House hostess was his niece Harriet Lane (1830-1903)
CHILDREN: Adopted children Mary Elizabeth and Harriet Rebecca.
PETS: Lara the Newfoundland, Punch the Toy Terrier, two eagles, and two canaries (one named Dick)
EDUCATION: Graduated from Dickinson College (1809)
RELIGION: Presbyterian
OCCUPATION: Lawyer, public official
OTHER GOVERNMENT POSITIONS: Member of Pennsylvania House of Representatives, 1815-16; Member of U.S. House of Representatives, 1821-31; Minister to Russia, 1832-34; U.S. Senator, 1834-45; Secretary of State, 1845-49 (under Polk); Minister to England, 1853-56
MILITARY SERVICE: Private, Pennsylvania Militia (1814)
PRESIDENTIAL SALARY: $25,000/year
DIED: June 1, 1868, at Wheatland (near Lancaster, Pennsylvania)
AGE AT DEATH: 77 years
CAUSE OF DEATH: Respiratory Failure
BURIED: Lancaster, Pennsylvania

James Buchanan

15th President of the United States (1857 – 1861)

James Buchanan was born in Cove Gap, Pennsylvania, and grew up in a family of farmers. He was the second of 11 children, and his father, James Sr., was a wealthy business owner and farmer.

As a young man, Buchanan attended Dickinson College in Carlisle, Pennsylvania, and later studied law. His excellent legal skills and his ability to negotiate complex legal disputes enabled him to become a prominent lawyer quickly in Lancaster, Pennsylvania.

During his presidency, Buchanan faced many challenges, including the escalating tensions between the North and South over slavery. Despite his efforts to prevent secession and maintain the Union, he could not prevent the outbreak of the Civil War.

One of Buchanan's most notable accomplishments as president was the negotiation of the Ostend Manifesto, which called for the acquisition of Cuba from Spain. Although the manifesto was unsuccessful, it showed Buchanan's commitment to expanding American territory.

After his presidency, Buchanan retired from politics and returned to his home in Lancaster. He continued to be active in public life, serving as a trustee of Dickinson College and supporting various charitable causes.

Buchanan also wrote extensively about his life and experiences, publishing several books on topics such as his travels to Europe and his experiences as a lawyer and politician. His memoirs, which were published posthumously, provide a unique perspective on the events of his life and the challenges he faced as a public figure.

Throughout his life, James Buchanan was known for his intellect, his commitment to public service, and his unwavering dedication to the principles of democracy and freedom. Although he faced many challenges and setbacks during his presidency, his legacy as a skilled lawyer, negotiator, and leader has endured to this day.

Fun Facts:

- Buchanan was fluent in both English and French.
- People often consider Harriet Lane, Buchanan's niece, one of the most popular and effective first ladies in American history because she served as his White House hostess.
- Buchanan's eccentric personal style included colorful clothing and a distinctive hairstyle. He also enjoyed fine wine and cigars.
- James Buchanan was the only president from Pennsylvania and earned the title "Father of Wheatland" for living there much of his life.
- Buchanan was the last president to be born in the 18th century.
- He was one of the oldest Presidents to take office, at 65.
- James Buchanan was the only president who never married and remains the only bachelor president. He had been engaged to a woman named Anne Colman, but she called off the engagement after a fight and died later that year in what some have said was a suicide.
- Buchanan received a dog, eagles, and elephants from his supporters.
- Someone tried to assassinate Buchanan by poisoning him at his own inauguration.

Abraham Lincoln

NICKNAME: "Honest Abe" and "Illinois Rail Splitter"
BORN: February 12, 1809, in Hardin (now Larue) County, Kentucky
POLITICAL PARTY: Republican and National Union
TERM OF OFFICE: March 4, 1861 – April 15, 1865
VICE PRESIDENT: Hannibal Hamlin (1861–1865), Andrew Johnson (1865)
AGE AT INAUGURATION: 52 years
NUMBER OF TERMS: One full term; assassinated: died 1 month and 11 days into second term, 1 day after being shot
PARENTS:
Thomas Lincoln
Nancy Hanks Lincoln
Sarah Bush Johnston Lincoln (Stepmother)
MARRIED: Mary Todd Lincoln (1818-1882), on November 4, 1842
CHILDREN: Robert, Edward, William, Thomas
PETS: Jack the turkey; goats named Nanny and Nanko; ponies; cats; dogs; pigs; a white rabbit
EDUCATION: No formal education
RELIGION: No formal affiliation
OCCUPATION: Lawyer, public official
OTHER GOVERNMENT POSITIONS: Elected to Illinois State Legislature, 1834; Member of U.S. House of Representatives, 1847-49
MILITARY SERVICE: Private and Captain, Illinois Militia (1832)
PRESIDENTIAL SALARY: $25,000/year
DIED: April 15, 1865, at Petersen's Boarding House in Washington, D.C.
AGE AT DEATH: 56 years
CAUSE OF DEATH: Gunshot Wound
BURIED: Springfield, Illinois

Abraham Lincoln

16th President of the United States (1861 – 1865)

Abraham Lincoln was born in a log cabin in rural Kentucky and grew up in poverty. His mother died when he was young, and he had a difficult relationship with his father. Despite his humble beginnings, Lincoln was determined to get an education, and he taught himself to read and write. He also worked on his family's farm and later as a laborer and shopkeeper.

In his early adult years, Lincoln worked as a lawyer, and he became involved in politics, serving in the Illinois state legislature and later in the U.S. House of Representatives. During this time, he gained a reputation as an effective and persuasive speaker.

During his presidency, Lincoln faced numerous challenges, including the secession of several Southern states and the outbreak of the Civil War. He is perhaps best known for his Emancipation Proclamation, which declared that all slaves in Confederate territory were to be set free. He also led the Union to victory in the Civil War, which ended in 1865 with the surrender of Confederate General Robert E. Lee.

After the war, Lincoln focused on the process of rebuilding the country, including efforts to heal the wounds of the conflict and to bring the South back into the Union. He also worked to extend voting rights and other civil liberties to African Americans.

Unfortunately, Lincoln's life was cut short when he was assassinated by John Wilkes Booth while attending a play at Ford's Theatre in Washington, D.C. Despite his untimely death, Lincoln's legacy lives on, and he is widely regarded as one of the greatest presidents in U.S. history.

Fun Facts:

- Lincoln was a skilled wrestler in his youth, winning 299 of 300 matches.
- He was the first president to sport a beard, which he grew after an 11-year-old girl wrote him a letter suggesting he would look better with one.
- Lincoln was a licensed bartender and owned a tavern in Springfield, Illinois, before he became president.
- He frequently suffered from intense and debilitating bouts of depression.
- Lincoln's bodyguard, John Parker, left his post at Ford's Theatre during the intermission of the play in which Lincoln was shot, leaving the president unguarded.
- Lincoln's dog Fido became famous for being the first presidential dog to be photographed.
- Despite being a great orator and writer, Lincoln's voice was high-pitched and somewhat nasally, and he was self-conscious about his appearance and speaking style.
- Lincoln was a licensed pilot of a steamboat on the Mississippi River before he entered politics.
- He is rumored to have had a premonition of his own death in a dream, in which he saw himself lying in state in the White House.
- Lincoln's pockets were found to contain two pairs of spectacles, a small velvet eyeglass cleaner, a watch fob, a linen handkerchief, a brown leather wallet, and a Confederate five-dollar bill at the time of his assassination.

Andrew Johnson (signature)

NICKNAME: "The Tennessee Tailor," "Sir Veto," and "The War Democrat"
BORN: December 29, 1808, in Raleigh, North Carolina
POLITICAL PARTY: National Union and Democratic
TERM OF OFFICE: April 15, 1865 – March 3, 1869
VICE PRESIDENT: None
AGE AT INAUGURATION: 56 years
NUMBER OF TERMS: One partial term (3 years, 10 months, and 17 days)
PARENTS:
Jacob Johnson
Mary McDonough Johnson
MARRIED: Eliza McCardle Johnson (1810-1876), on May 5, 1827
CHILDREN: Martha, Charles, Mary, Robert, Andrew Jr.
PETS: No official pets, but he did feed the mice in the White House
EDUCATION: No formal education
RELIGION: No formal affiliation
OCCUPATION: Tailor, public official
OTHER GOVERNMENT POSITIONS: Served as Alderman of Greeneville, Tennessee, 1830-33; Elected Mayor of Greeneville, Tennessee, 1834; Member of Tennessee State Legislature, 1835-43; Member of U.S. House of Representatives, 1843-53; Governor of Tennessee, 1853-57; U.S. Senator, 1857-62; Military Governor of Tennessee, 1862-65; Vice President, 1865 (under Lincoln); U.S. Senator, 1875
MILITARY SERVICE: Brigadier General, U.S. Army (1862-1865)
PRESIDENTIAL SALARY: $25,000/year
DIED: July 31, 1875, in Carter's Station, Tennessee
AGE AT DEATH: 66 years
CAUSE OF DEATH: Stroke
BURIED: Greeneville, Tennessee

Andrew Johnson

17th President of the United States (1865 – 1869)

Andrew Johnson was born in Raleigh, North Carolina, and spent most of his childhood working alongside his father as a tailor's apprentice. He did not receive a formal education, but he learned how to read and write from his mother.

As a young man, Johnson moved to Tennessee and eventually became involved in politics. He served as a member of the Tennessee state legislature and later as a U.S. Congressman and Senator.

During his presidency, Johnson's most significant accomplishment was the passage of the Reconstruction Acts of 1867. These laws aimed to rebuild the Southern states after the Civil War by granting citizenship and voting rights to African Americans, creating new state governments, and enforcing new civil rights laws.

Johnson's presidency provoked controversy and conflict with Congress, leading to his impeachment. He was the first U.S. president to face impeachment, but the Senate ultimately acquitted him.

After his presidency, Johnson returned to Tennessee and remained active in politics. He was elected to the U.S. Senate in 1875 but died soon after taking office.

Johnson was a skilled orator and advocated for states' rights and against secession before the Civil War.

Fun Facts:

- Andrew Johnson was the only U.S. president to have been a tailor by trade. Andrew Johnson never received a formal education and apprenticed as a tailor at a young age.
- He was the only senator from a seceding state (Tennessee) to remain loyal to the Union during the Civil War. This led to his selection as Lincoln's vice president in 1864.
- Johnson's frequent drunkenness led to several embarrassing incidents during his presidency, including a series of drunken speeches.
- He was the first president to be impeached by the House of Representatives. The impeachment stemmed from Johnson's resistance to the Reconstruction policies put in place after the Civil War.
- Johnson was a staunch supporter of states' rights and opposed many of the measures taken by Congress to enforce equal rights for African Americans during Reconstruction. Congress overrode his veto of the Civil Rights Act of 1866.
- Johnson was known for his stubbornness and refusal to compromise. This led to conflicts with both Congress and his own cabinet members.
- He once said, "I am sworn to uphold the Constitution as Andrew Johnson understands it and interprets it."
- Johnson was the first President to grant a general amnesty to all former Confederates who pledged loyalty to the United States.
- Johnson was the first President to serve without a Vice President for his entire term in office.
- Andrew Johnson was often criticized for his unconventional approach to the presidency, including his tendency to speak directly to the public rather than through Congress.

Ulysses S. Grant

18th President of the United States (1869 – 1877)

Ulysses S. Grant was born in Ohio in 1822 and grew up in a family of modest means. Grant's father was a tanner and Grant assisted in running his family's farm in a small town.

As a young man, Grant was an above-average student and showed an aptitude for mathematics. He excelled in horseback riding and found solace in the outdoors.

In 1843, Grant graduated from the United States Military Academy at West Point, where he showed an aptitude for military strategy and leadership. After serving in the Mexican-American War, he left the military in 1854 to pursue civilian life.

When the Civil War broke out in 1861, Grant rejoined the Union Army and quickly rose through the ranks. He is widely regarded as one of the most skilled military commanders in American history, and his victories at battles like Vicksburg and Chattanooga were crucial to the Union's eventual victory.

During his presidency, Grant oversaw significant reforms in government, including the passage of the 15th Amendment, which granted voting rights to African American men. He also worked to promote civil rights and to enforce laws protecting African Americans in the South.

After leaving office, Grant embarked on a world tour and wrote a memoir of his experiences during the Civil War, which became a bestseller. His business partner swindled him out of his savings, and he was later diagnosed with throat cancer.

Despite his illness, Grant continued to work on his memoirs, which he hoped would provide financial security for his family after his death. He completed the book just days before he passed away in 1885, and it is still considered one of the most important works of American military history.

Fun Facts:

- Ulysses S. Grant's real name was Hiram Ulysses Grant. A benefactor mistakenly listed him as "Ulysses S. Grant" instead of "Ulysses H. Grant."
- He was a man of few words and disliked public speaking.
- Grant was an animal lover and had several pets during his lifetime, including a black horse he named Jeff Davis (named after the president of the Confederacy).
- Grant was arrested in 1872 for speeding on his horse. He was racing his horse through town when a police officer pulled him over and took him to jail. Grant paid a $20 bond but didn't show up in court.
- Grant often indulged in his love of cigars in public. He once received a gift of 10,000 cigars from a grateful admirer.
- Critics consider his memoirs, which he wrote while suffering from the throat cancer, one of the greatest works of American literature.
- He established Yellowstone National Park in 1872.
- Grant received many demerits for his unkempt uniforms during his days at West Point, and his distaste for wearing army uniforms continued throughout his life.
- When Robert E. Lee surrendered to bring the Civil War officially to an end, Grant allowed the Confederate soldiers to keep their weapons and their horses.

NICKNAME: "Hero of Appomattox," "'Unconditional Surrender' Grant," "The Galena Tanner," "Sam," "Old Reliable," "The Butcher," "The Silent Man," "The Rock of Chickamauga," and "The Lion of the Potomac"
BORN: April 27, 1822, in Point Pleasant, Ohio
POLITICAL PARTY: Republican
TERM OF OFFICE: March 4, 1869 – March 4, 1877
VICE PRESIDENT: Schuyler Colfax (1869–1873), Henry Wilson (1873–1875)
AGE AT INAUGURATION: 46 years
NUMBER OF TERMS: Two full terms
PARENTS:
Jesse Root Grant
Hannah Simpson Grant
MARRIED: Julia Boggs Dent Grant (1826-1902), on August 22, 1848
CHILDREN: Frederick, Ulysses Jr., Ellen, Jesse
PETS: Faithful, a Newfoundland; horses named Jeff Davis, Julia, Jennie, Mary, Butcher Boy, Cincinnatus, Egypt, and St. Louis; ponies named Reb and Billy Button; pigs; dogs; a parrot; roosters
EDUCATION: Graduated from the U.S. Military Academy in West Point, N.Y. (1843)
RELIGION: Methodist
OCCUPATION: Soldier
OTHER GOVERNMENT POSITIONS: None
MILITARY SERVICE: Captain, U.S. Army (1839-1854); General, U.S. Army (1861-1869)
PRESIDENTIAL SALARY: $25,000/year (increased to $50,000/year in 1873)
DIED: July 23, 1885, in Mount McGregor, New York
AGE AT DEATH: 63 years
CAUSE OF DEATH: Cancer
BURIED: New York, New York

Rutherford B. Hayes (signature)

NICKNAME: "The Great Unknown," "Rutherfraud," "His Fraudulency," and "Old 8 to 7"
BORN: October 4, 1822, in Delaware, Ohio
POLITICAL PARTY: Republican
TERM OF OFFICE: March 4, 1877 – March 3, 1881
VICE PRESIDENT: William A. Wheeler
AGE AT INAUGURATION: 54 years
NUMBER OF TERMS: One full term
PARENTS:
Rutherford Hayes
Sophia Birchard Hayes
MARRIED: Lucy Ware Webb Hayes (1831-1889), on December 30, 1852
CHILDREN: Sardis, James, Rutherford, Joseph, George, Frances, Scott, Manning
PETS: Dogs: Jet, hunting dogs Juno and Shep, Hector the Newfoundland, Duke the English mastiff, Grim the greyhound, Otis the miniature schnauzer, Dot the cocker spaniel; Cats: Piccolomini, and Siamese cats named Siam and Miss Pussy; a goat, four canaries, pedigreed Jersey cows, and several carriage horses
EDUCATION: Graduated from Kenyon College (1842) and Harvard Law School (1845)
RELIGION: No formal affiliation
OCCUPATION: Lawyer, public official
OTHER GOVERNMENT POSITIONS: Member of U.S. House of Representatives, 1865-67; Governor of Ohio, 1868-72; Governor of Ohio, 1876-77
MILITARY SERVICE: Major General, U.S. Volunteer Army (1861-1865)
PRESIDENTIAL SALARY: $50,000/year
DIED: January 17, 1893, at Spiegel Grove in Fremont, Ohio
AGE AT DEATH: 70 years
CAUSE OF DEATH: Heart Attack
BURIED: Fremont, Ohio

Rutherford B. Hayes

19th President of the United States (1877 – 1881)

Rutherford B. Hayes' parents fled the poor economy of New England and resettled in Delaware, Ohio. He was named for his father and grandfather.

Before his presidency, he served as a lawyer and politician. He was a member of the Whig Party before joining the Republican Party. He served as a major general in the Union Army during the American Civil War.

During his presidency, he restored prestige to the presidency and strengthened the Republican Party sufficiently to win the election of 1880. He also helped heal some of the wounds left by the Civil War. His administration saw the end of post-Civil War Reconstruction. He is credited with restoring citizens' faith in the presidency through his efforts to curb corruption that had become rampant in government.

After his presidency, he continued to struggle for equal educational opportunities for all children. He also was active in the prison reform movement. His major emphasis was on universal tax-supported public education. He believed that education would improve the nation morally and materially and labored constantly to improve educational opportunities for students from grade school to graduate school.

Fun Facts:

- Despite having no military experience, a 40-year-old Hayes left his law practice to join the Union Army in 1861 during the Civil War, participating in several major battles and was wounded five times.
- The first Siamese kitten to arrive in America was owned by Hayes.
- The disputed 1876 U.S. presidential election was settled through the Compromise of 1877, an agreement where Hayes was granted the last 20 electoral votes to win the election on the condition that he removed federal troops from the South.
- Hayes made history by appointing Frederick Douglass, the first African American to receive Senate confirmation for a Presidential appointment, as marshal of Washington, D.C.
- Hayes started the White House Easter egg hunt in 1878.
- Hayes signed the bill making February 22nd a federal holiday in 1879, almost a century after the birth of George Washington.
- Hayes was the first U.S. President to advocate for a merit-based system for federal job appointments instead of the corrupt Spoils System.
- While Hayes is not widely celebrated in the U.S., he is highly regarded in Paraguay for settling a territorial dispute in their favor.
- Hayes was the first law school graduate president, from Harvard.
- Hayes and his wife were both interested in higher education for women and worked to promote women's education during his presidency.
- Although the first lady was known as "Lemonade Lucy" for not drinking alcohol, it was Hayes who banned all alcoholic beverages at the presidential mansion.
- He was the first president to have electric lights in the White House.
- Hayes was the first president to travel outside the country while in office (to visit Canada in 1878).

James A. Garfield (signature)

NICKNAME: "The Preacher President," "The Educator President," "Boatman Jim," "The Canal Boy," "The Scholar-President," and "Old Whiskers"
BORN: November 19, 1831, in Orange, Ohio
POLITICAL PARTY: Republican
TERM OF OFFICE: March 4, 1881 – September 19, 1881
VICE PRESIDENT: Chester Alan Arthur
AGE AT INAUGURATION: 49 years
NUMBER OF TERMS: Assassinated: died 6 months and 15 days into term, 79 days after being shot
PARENTS:
Abram Garfield
Eliza Ballou Garfield
MARRIED: Lucretia Rudolph Garfield (1832-1918), on November 11, 1858
CHILDREN: Eliza, Harry, James, Mary, Irvin, Abram, Edward
PETS: Kit the horse; Veto the dog; fish
EDUCATION: Attended Western Reserve Eclectic Institute (now Hiram College); Graduated from Williams College (1856)
RELIGION: Disciples of Christ
OCCUPATION: Teacher, public official
OTHER GOVERNMENT POSITIONS: Member of Ohio State Senate, 1859-61; Member of U.S. House of Representatives, 1863-80; Elected to U.S. Senate, 1880
MILITARY SERVICE: Major General, U.S. Army (1861-1863)
PRESIDENTIAL SALARY: $50,000/year
DIED: September 19, 1881, in Elberon, New Jersey
AGE AT DEATH: 49 years
CAUSE OF DEATH: Gunshot Wound
BURIED: Cleveland, Ohio

James A. Garfield

20th President of the United States (1881)

James A. Garfield was born in Cuyahoga County, Ohio. He was the last of five children born to Abram and Eliza Garfield. His father died when he was only two years old, leaving his mother to raise the family on her own. Despite this, Garfield was an excellent student and showed an early aptitude for learning.

Garfield attended Western Reserve Eclectic Institute (now known as Hiram College), where he excelled academically and became interested in the abolitionist movement. He later went on to Williams College in Massachusetts, where he studied classical languages and was elected to the Phi Beta Kappa society. After graduating, he returned to Ohio and became a professor at his alma mater, Western Reserve Eclectic Institute.

In 1859, Garfield was elected to the Ohio State Senate, where he became known for his eloquence and support of the Union during the Civil War. He later resigned from the Senate to join the Union Army, where he quickly rose through the ranks to become a brigadier general. Garfield played a significant role in several battles, including the Battle of Middle Creek and the Battle of Chickamauga.

After the war, Garfield was elected to the U.S. House of Representatives, where he served for nearly 18 years. During this time, he became known for his support of civil rights for African Americans and his opposition to corruption in government. He was also instrumental in the passage of the 14th Amendment to the Constitution, which granted citizenship to all persons born or naturalized in the United States, including former slaves.

In 1880, Garfield was elected to the presidency of the United States, defeating Democrat Winfield Scott Hancock. During his brief presidency, he accomplished several significant feats. He appointed a cabinet of highly qualified individuals, including Secretary of State James G. Blaine, who was instrumental in expanding American influence in Latin America.

Unfortunately, Garfield's presidency was cut short when he was assassinated just six months after taking office. On July 2nd, 1881, while waiting for a train at the Baltimore and Potomac Railroad Station in Washington, D.C., he was shot twice by Charles J. Guiteau, a disgruntled office-seeker who believed he deserved a government position. Garfield survived the initial shooting but suffered for several months before ultimately dying on September 19th, 1881, due to an infection caused by the bullet wounds.

Garfield's death shocked the nation, and his legacy as a statesman and scholar was cemented. He was the second U.S. president to be assassinated, following Abraham Lincoln. Today, Garfield is remembered for his support of civil rights and his efforts to combat government corruption, as well as his tragic death.

Fun Facts:

- Garfield was the first left-handed President of the United States.
- He was the last president born in a log cabin.
- He originally wanted to sail the open seas as a s sailor
- Garfield's mother named him after a famous Presbyterian minister who was known for his piety and moral values.
- He was nicknamed the "Preacher President" due to his powerful speaking skills.

Chester A. Arthur

21st President of the United States (1881 – 1885)

NICKNAME: "Elegant Arthur," "The Gentleman Boss," "Prince Arthur," "Chet," and "The Dude President"
BORN: October 5, 1829, in Fairfield, Vermont
POLITICAL PARTY: Republican
TERM OF OFFICE: September 19, 1881 – March 4, 1885
VICE PRESIDENT: None
AGE AT INAUGURATION: 51 years
NUMBER OF TERMS: One partial term (3 years, 5 months, and 13 days)
PARENTS:
William Arthur
Malvina Stone Arthur
MARRIED: Ellen Lewis Herndon Arthur (1837-1880), on October 25, 1859
CHILDREN: William, Chester, Ellen
PETS: Rabbit and three horses
EDUCATION: Graduated from Union College (1848)
RELIGION: Episcopalian
OCCUPATION: Lawyer, public official
OTHER GOVERNMENT POSITIONS: Vice president, 1881 (under Garfield)
MILITARY SERVICE: Brigadier General, New York Militia (1857-1863): Assignments during Civil War included Quartermaster General of the New York Militia (July 27, 1862 – January 1, 1863); Inspector General of the New York Militia (April 14, 1862 – July 12, 1862); Engineer-in-Chief of the New York Militia (January 1, 1861 – January 1, 1863)
PRESIDENTIAL SALARY: $50,000/year
DIED: November 18, 1886, in New York, New York
AGE AT DEATH: 57 years
CAUSE OF DEATH: Stroke
BURIED: Menands, New York

Chester A. Arthur was born in Vermont and spent his early years in upstate New York. As a child, he was known for his studious nature and was a top student in his local school district. He attended Union College in Schenectady, New York, where he excelled in his studies.

Before his presidency, Arthur was a successful lawyer and had a reputation for being a skilled litigator. He was known for his attention to detail and his ability to win over juries with his eloquence. President James Garfield appointed him as the Collector of the Port of New York and charged him with collecting customs duties on imported goods.

During his presidency, Arthur is credited with modernizing the United States Navy. He signed the Naval Appropriations Act of 1883, which provided funding for new ships and improved the infrastructure of naval bases. He also signed the Pendleton Civil Service Reform Act which created a merit-based system for government jobs and helped to reduce corruption in government.

After his presidency, Arthur returned to private law practice and continued to be an active member of the Republican Party. He was involved in the founding of the New York State Bar Association and served as its president. He also served as a trustee of his alma mater, Union College.

Arthur's legacy also includes his efforts to improve the lives of African Americans. He signed the Civil Rights Act of 1875, which outlawed racial discrimination in public accommodations. While the law was later declared unconstitutional by the Supreme Court, it marked a significant step towards equal rights for African Americans.

Chester A. Arthur devoted himself to public service and improving the country he loved throughout his life.

Fun Facts:

- Arthur owned 80 pairs of pants and changed them several times a day.
- He was the first president to take the oath of office in a private home, rather than the Capitol building.
- Arthur belonged to the "Gilded Age" Republicans, who were notorious for their extravagant lifestyles and political corruption.
- He was known for his dapper style, often sporting a top hat and cane.
- Arthur suffered from Bright's disease, a kidney disorder that was eventually fatal.
- He tried to pass a civil service reform bill, but Congress largely watered it down.
- Arthur was a widower when he became president and never remarried during his time in office.
- He was a supporter of civil service reform, despite his reputation as a product of the political machine.
- Throughout Arthur's political career, rumors circulated he had been born in Bedford, Quebec, Canada, although nobody ever proved it. Many Canadians asserted Arthur was probably a British subject and citizen of Lower Canada, born in Dunham Flats, Quebec, close to the Vermont border.

Grover Cleveland (signature)

NICKNAME: "Uncle Jumbo," "Big Steve," "Veto Mayor," "The Veto President," "Grover the Good," "The Stuffed Prophet," "The Man of Destiny," "The Honest President," and "The Last Jeffersonian"
BORN: March 18, 1837, in Caldwell, New Jersey
POLITICAL PARTY: Democratic
TERM OF OFFICE: March 4, 1885 – March 4, 1889
VICE PRESIDENT: Thomas Hendricks
AGE AT INAUGURATION: 47 years
NUMBER OF TERMS: Two full terms (non-consecutive)
PARENTS:
Richard Falley Cleveland
Anne Neal Cleveland
MARRIED: Frances Folsom Cleveland (1864-1947), on June 2, 1886
CHILDREN: Oscar, Ruth, Esther, Richard, Francis
PETS: Dogs: Collie, Gallagher the cocker spaniel, a collie, 3 dachhunds, foxhounds, Kay the St. Bernard, Hector the black French poodle; Birds: Canaries, mockingbirds, and Shawlneck game chickens; ponies; hundreds of imported fish (including Japanese goldfish as well as paradise fish)
EDUCATION: No formal education
RELIGION: Presbyterian
OCCUPATION: Lawyer, public official
MILITARY SERVICE: None
OTHER GOVERNMENT POSITIONS: Sheriff of Erie County, NY, 1870-73; Mayor of Buffalo, NY, 1882; Governor of New York, 1883-85
PRESIDENTIAL SALARY: $50,000/year
DIED: June 24, 1908, in Princeton, New Jersey
AGE AT DEATH: 71 years
CAUSE OF DEATH: Heart Attack
BURIED: Princeton, New Jersey

Grover Cleveland

22nd and 24th President of the United States (1885 – 1889, 1893 - 1897)

Grover Cleveland was born in New Jersey and grew up in upstate New York. His father was a Presbyterian minister, and Cleveland was the fifth of nine children. He had a relatively uneventful childhood, marked by his family's financial struggles and his own struggle with obesity.

Before his presidency, Cleveland had a successful career as a lawyer and politician. He was elected mayor of Buffalo, New York, in 1881, and gained a reputation as a reformer who fought against corruption and patronage. He was later elected governor of New York in 1882, where he continued his efforts to clean up politics and improve government efficiency.

During his presidency, Cleveland was known for his commitment to fiscal conservatism and government reform. He vetoed hundreds of bills that he believed were unnecessary or wasteful, earning him the nickname "Veto President." He also signed the Interstate Commerce Act of 1887, which regulated railroad rates and helped to prevent unfair business practices.

After his presidency, Cleveland continued to be involved in politics and public service. He spoke out against the annexation of Hawaii and the Spanish-American War, and supported the establishment of the Hague Tribunal for international arbitration. He also served as a trustee of Princeton University and worked to establish a national park system.

Overall, Grover Cleveland was a principled and effective leader who dedicated his life to improving government and promoting reform. His legacy continues to inspire public servants today.

Fun Facts:

- Grover Cleveland was the only U.S. president to serve two non-consecutive terms in office. He served as the 22nd president from 1885 to 1889, and then as the 24th president from 1893 to 1897.
- Cleveland was the only president to get married in the White House. He was 49 years old when he married Frances Folsom, who was just 21. They had five children together.
- He was the first president to have a child born in the White House. In 1893, his wife gave birth to a daughter, Esther, in the White House.
- He had a growth removed from the roof of his mouth in secret, to avoid causing concern among the public. The surgery was performed aboard a yacht, with only a few trusted aides present.
- Cleveland had a reputation for being stubborn, which made it difficult for him to work with Congress.
- He was the first Democratic president since the Civil War, and he was known for his support of states' rights and limited government. He was also opposed to tariffs, which he believed were unfair to consumers.
- He once vetoed a bill that would have provided $10,000 in seed money for a Texas state fair. He argued it was not the government's job to provide funding for such events.
- Cleveland's real first name was Stephen, but he went by his middle name, Grover.
- He once had a cartoon character named after him called "Uncle Jumbo".

Benj. Harrison

NICKNAME: "Little Ben," "The Human Iceberg," "Kid Gloves Harrison," "The Centennial President," "The Hoosier President," "The Front Porch Campaigner," "The Blue Hen's Chicken," and "The White House Iceberg"
BORN: August 20, 1833, in North Bend, Ohio
POLITICAL PARTY: Republican
TERM OF OFFICE: March 4, 1889 – March 4, 1893
VICE PRESIDENT: Levi P. Morton
AGE AT INAUGURATION: 55 years
NUMBER OF TERMS: One full term
PARENTS:
John Scott Harrison
Elizabeth Ramsey Irwin Harrison
MARRIED: Caroline Lavinia Scott Harrison (1832-1892), on October 20, 1853; Mary Scott Lord Dimmick (1858-1948), on April 6, 1896
CHILDREN: Russell, Mary, Elizabeth, and an unnamed daughter
PETS: Dash the collie; Whiskers the goat; dogs; Mr. Reciprocity and Mr. Protection the oppossums.
EDUCATION: Graduated from Miami University, Oxford, Ohio (1852)
RELIGION: Presbyterian
OCCUPATION: Lawyer, public official
MILITARY SERVICE: Brevet Brigadier General, U.S. Volunteer Army (1862-1865)
OTHER GOVERNMENT POSITIONS: U.S. Senator, 1881-87
PRESIDENTIAL SALARY: $50,000/year
DIED: March 13, 1901, in Indianapolis, Indiana
AGE AT DEATH: 67 years
CAUSE OF DEATH: Pneumonia
BURIED: Indianapolis, Indiana

Benjamin Harrison

23rd President of the United States (1889 – 1893)

Benjamin Harrison was born into a prominent political family in Ohio and grew up in Indianapolis, Indiana. His grandfather, William Henry Harrison, was the ninth President of the United States, and his father, John Scott Harrison, served as a U.S. Representative.

As a child, Harrison was highly educated and attended Miami University in Ohio, where he studied law. After graduation, he moved to Indianapolis and established a successful law practice.

During his presidency, Harrison was known for his commitment to expanding the country's economic and military power. He signed the Sherman Antitrust Act into law, which was designed to prevent monopolies and promote fair competition. He also oversaw the passage of the McKinley Tariff Act, which raised tariffs on imported goods to protect American industries.

Harrison's administration was also notable for its foreign policy achievements. He negotiated a treaty with Hawaii that established a naval base at Pearl Harbor, which would become an important strategic location for the United States during World War II. He also presided over the first Pan-American Conference, which brought together leaders from across the Americas to promote cooperation and trade.

After leaving office, Harrison continued to be involved in politics and served as a delegate to the Republican National Convention. He also remained active in his legal practice and argued several cases before the U.S. Supreme Court.

Besides his political and legal career, Harrison was also a dedicated philanthropist. He served as the first president of the Board of Trustees of Purdue University and helped establish the John Herron Art Institute in Indianapolis. He was also a leader in the Presbyterian Church and served as an elder in his congregation.

Overall, Benjamin Harrison was a highly accomplished individual who made significant contributions to the United States during his lifetime.

Fun Facts:

- Benjamin Harrison was the only U.S. president who had a grandfather who was also a U.S. president. His grandfather was William Henry Harrison, who served as the ninth President of the United States.
- Harrison was the first president with electricity in the White House but feared touching the switches.
- He was known for being very formal and stiff in public, and Harrison was often criticized for his lack of charisma.
- Harrison installed the first Christmas tree in the White House.
- He was also the first president to have his voice recorded. In 1889, Harrison made a recording on a phonograph that is stored at the Library of Congress.
- He was the first president to attend the opening ceremony of the World's Columbian Exposition, which was held in Chicago in 1893.
- Harrison won the election of 1888 by winning the most electoral votes, but his opponent, Grover Cleveland, won the popular vote.
- Despite his father's warning about the pressures of a life in politics, Harrison's wife encouraged his political ambitions.

CHAPTER 4

PROGRESSIVE ERA (1896–1932)

The Progressive Era (1896-1932) was a period of significant social, economic, and political reform in the United States. It was a time of great change as Americans responded to the challenges of industrialization and urbanization. Here is a detailed chronology of events within each era:

1. Early Progressive Era (1896-1900)
    - 1896: Plessy v. Ferguson ruling upholds the "separate but equal" doctrine for public facilities.
    - 1897: National Association of Colored Women founded.
    - 1898: Spanish-American War; U.S. gains Puerto Rico, Guam, and the Philippines.
2. Progressive Era in Full Swing (1901-1917)
    - 1901: Theodore Roosevelt becomes President after the assassination of William McKinley.
    - 1902: Coal Strike of 1902 ends after Roosevelt intervenes.
    - 1903: Women's Trade Union League founded.
    - 1904: Roosevelt wins re-election, becomes first president to use the term "muckrakers" to describe investigative journalists.
    - 1906: Pure Food and Drug Act and Meat Inspection Act passed.
    - 1908: Muller v. Oregon ruling upholds a law limiting women to ten hours of work per day.
    - 1909: National Association for the Advancement of Colored People (NAACP) founded.
    - 1911: Triangle Shirtwaist Factory Fire in New York City kills 146 garment workers, leading to stricter workplace safety regulations.
    - 1912: Woodrow Wilson wins presidential election after a split in the Republican Party.
    - 1913: 16th Amendment to the U.S. Constitution ratified, allowing Congress to levy a federal income tax.
    - 1914: Clayton Antitrust Act passed, strengthening federal authority to regulate corporations.
    - 1916: National Park Service established.
3. World War I and the End of the Progressive Era (1917-1932)
    - 1917: U.S. enters World War I on the side of the Allies.
    - 1918: Armistice signed, ending World War I.
    - 1919: 18th Amendment to the U.S. Constitution ratified, prohibiting the manufacture, sale, and transportation of alcohol.
    - 1920: 19th Amendment to the U.S. Constitution ratified, granting women the right to vote.
    - 1920s: Ku Klux Klan reaches the peak of its power.
    - 1929: Stock market crash and beginning of the Great Depression.
    - 1932: Franklin D. Roosevelt elected president and launches the New Deal, a series of programs designed to provide relief, recovery, and reform during the Great Depression.

The American people demanded change in all aspects of life during the Progressive Era and pushed for government action to make those changes a reality. The Progressive Era's legacy can still be seen in many of the reforms and institutions that continue to shape American society today.

NICKNAME: "Idol of Ohio," "The Major", "The Napoleon of Protection," "The Advance Agent of Prosperity," "The Ohio Eagle," and "The Last Veteran President"
BORN: January 29, 1843, in Niles, Ohio
POLITICAL PARTY: Republican
TERM OF OFFICE: March 4, 1897 – September 14, 1901
VICE PRESIDENT: Garret A. Hobart (1897–1899), Theodore Roosevelt (1901)
AGE AT INAUGURATION: 54 years
NUMBER OF TERMS: One full term; assassinated: died 6 months and 10 days into second term, 8 days after being shot
PARENTS:
William McKinley
Nancy Campbell Allison McKinley
MARRIED: Ida Saxton (1847-1907), on January 25, 1871
CHILDREN: Katherine, Ida
PETS: Valeriano Weylrer and Engrique DeLome the cats (named after Spanish general Valerian Wyler and Spanish ambassador Enrique Dupuy de Lome), Washington Post the double yellow-headed bird, and roosters
EDUCATION: Attended Allegheny College
RELIGION: Methodist
OCCUPATION: Lawyer, public official
OTHER GOVERNMENT POSITIONS: Member of U.S. House of Representatives, 1877-91; Governor of Ohio, 1892-96
MILITARY SERVICE: Brevet Major, U.S. Volunteer Army (1861-1865)
PRESIDENTIAL SALARY: $50,000/year
DIED: September 14, 1901, in Buffalo, New York
AGE AT DEATH: 58 years
CAUSE OF DEATH: Gunshot Wound
BURIED: Canton, Ohio

William McKinley

25th President of the United States (1897 – 1901)

William McKinley was born in Niles, Ohio, in 1843. He was the seventh child of a family of nine children. McKinley's father, William McKinley Sr., was a businessman, while his mother, Nancy Allison McKinley, was a homemaker.

As a child, McKinley was a good student, and he was particularly interested in history and politics. He attended a local school in Niles, and later attended Allegheny College in Pennsylvania, although he did not graduate.

Before he became president, McKinley served as a soldier in the Union Army during the Civil War. He was eventually promoted to the rank of major, and he saw action in several battles, including the Battle of Antietam and the Battle of Winchester.

During his presidency, McKinley is perhaps best known for his leadership during the Spanish-American War. He mobilized the United States military and lead the country to victory over Spain. This victory led to the acquisition of several new territories, including Puerto Rico and the Philippines.

Another notable accomplishment of McKinley's presidency was the passage of the Gold Standard Act in 1900. This legislation established the gold standard as the official monetary policy of the United States, and it helped to stabilize the economy.

After his presidency, McKinley continued to be active in politics. He served as an advocate for the gold standard, and he also worked to improve relations between the United States and Latin America. Sadly, his life was cut short when he was assassinated in 1901 by Leon Czolgosz, an anarchist who disagreed with McKinley's policies.

Overall, William McKinley was a dedicated public servant who worked tirelessly to promote the interests of the United States, both at home and abroad. His leadership during the Spanish-American War and his advocacy for the gold standard are just two examples of the many ways in which he contributed to American society.

Fun Facts:

- William McKinley was the first U.S. president to ride in an automobile. In 1899, he rode in a Stanley Steamer car during a visit to the White House.
- He was known for being very superstitious. McKinley always carried a lucky red carnation in his lapel.
- He was the last U.S. president to have served in the Civil War. McKinley served in the Union Army and was promoted to the rank of brevet major.
- McKinley was the first U.S. president to campaign by telephone. In the1896 presidential campaign, he telephoned voters in different parts of the country.
- McKinley's wife, Ida, suffered from epilepsy and frequently could not perform her official duties as First Lady. This led to some speculation and rumors about her mental health.
- He was the first U.S. president to have his inauguration filmed.
- McKinley was the first U.S. president to appear on a U.S. coin during his lifetime. His portrait appeared on the 1901 Pan-American Exposition gold dollar, which was minted just a few months before his assassination.
- Unlike many of the presidents of that era, McKinley did not have a beard.

Theodore Roosevelt (signature)

NICKNAME: "TR," "Trust-Buster,"
BORN: October 27, 1858, in New York, New York
POLITICAL PARTY: Republican
TERM OF OFFICE: September 14, 1901 – March 4, 1909
VICE PRESIDENT: Charles W. Fairbanks (1905–1909)
AGE AT INAUGURATION: 42 years
NUMBER OF TERMS: One partial term (3 years, 5 months, and 18 days), followed by one full term
PARENTS:
Theodore Roosevelt
Martha Bulloch Roosevelt
MARRIED: Alice Hathaway Lee (1861-1884), on October 27, 1880; Edith Kermit Carow Roosevelt (1861-1948), on December 2, 1886
CHILDREN: With Alice Hathaway Lee: Alice; With Eidit Kermit Carow: Theodore Jr., Kermit, Ethel, Archibald, Quentin
PETS: Snakes, dogs, cats, a badger, birds, guinea pigs, and more
EDUCATION: Graduated from Harvard College (1880)
RELIGION: Dutch Reformed
OCCUPATION: Author, lawyer, public official
OTHER GOVERNMENT POSITIONS: Member of New York State Assembly, 1882-84; Member of Civil Service Commission, 1889-95; Assistant Secretary of the Navy, 1895-97; Governor of New York, 1898-1900; Vice President, 1901 (under McKinley)
MILITARY SERVICE: Captain, New York National Guard (1882-1886); Colonel, U.S. Volunteer Army (1898)
PRESIDENTIAL SALARY: $50,000/year
DIED: January 6, 1919, in Oyster Bay, New York
AGE AT DEATH: 60 years
CAUSE OF DEATH: Pulmonary Embolism
BURIED: Oyster Bay, New York

Theodore Roosevelt

26th President of the United States (1901 – 1909)

Theodore Roosevelt, known as Teddy, was a remarkable American statesman, politician, conservationist, naturalist, and writer. He was born in New York City into a wealthy family and grew up in a privileged household. As a child, Roosevelt was sickly, suffering from severe asthma. His father encouraged him to engage in physical activities such as boxing and hunting, which helped him develop his strength and confidence.

During his presidency, Roosevelt was a progressive reformer, advocating for labor rights, consumer protection, and environmental conservation. He signed several landmark pieces of legislation, including the Pure Food and Drug Act, which regulated the food and pharmaceutical industries, and the Antiquities Act, which gave the president the power to protect public lands by creating national monuments.

After leaving office in 1909, Roosevelt continued to be a force in American politics. He embarked on a world tour and then became involved in efforts to promote conservation and environmental protection. In 1912, he made an unsuccessful bid for the presidency as the candidate of the Progressive Party, which he had helped to create.

In addition to his political and environmental accomplishments, Roosevelt was also a prolific author and wrote several books, including *The Naval War of 1812* and *The Rough Riders*, which detailed his experiences during the Spanish-American War.

Overall, his tireless dedication to public service, his commitment to conservation and environmental protection, and his determination to overcome adversity and make a positive impact on the world characterized Roosevelt's life.

Fun Facts:

- Roosevelt was an avid collector of natural specimens, including birds, mammals, insects, and plants. He even had a small museum in the White House and used his hunting expeditions to gather specimens for his collection.
- Shot during a 1912 campaign speech, Roosevelt persisted and delivered his scheduled speech despite the bullet lodged in his chest.
- Roosevelt was the first U.S. president to travel outside of the country while in office. In 1906, he visited Panama to inspect the progress of the construction of the Panama Canal.
- Roosevelt was a strong advocate for conservation and established many national parks and wildlife refuges during his presidency. He also helped to establish the U.S. Forest Service and signed the Antiquities Act, which allowed him to designate national monuments.
- Roosevelt was the first U.S. president to win a Nobel Peace Prize, which he was awarded in 1906 for his role in negotiating the end of the Russo-Japanese War.
- Roosevelt was a prolific writer and wrote over 40 books in his lifetime.
- In his book, *The Wilderness Hunter*, which was published in 1893, Roosevelt wrote about another hunter having an encounter with Bigfoot.
- As a child, Roosevelt saw the funeral procession of Abraham Lincoln.

W. H. Taft (signature)

NICKNAME: "Big Bill," "The Trust Buster," "Old Bill," "Sleepy Bill," "The Fat Fellow," and "Chief Justice"
BORN: September 15, 1857, in Cincinnati, Ohio
POLITICAL PARTY: Republican
TERM OF OFFICE: March 4, 1909 – March 4, 1913
VICE PRESIDENT: James S. Sherman
AGE AT INAUGURATION: 51 years
NUMBER OF TERMS: One full term
PARENTS:
Alphonso Taft
Louisa Maria Torrey Taft
MARRIED: Helen Herron (1861-1943), on June 19, 1886
CHILDREN: Robert, Helen, Charles
PETS: Caruso the dog (a gift for Taft's daughter Helen from opera singer Enrico Caruso) and cows Mooly Wooly and Pauline Wayne
EDUCATION: Graduated from Yale College (1878); Cincinnati Law School (1880)
RELIGION: Unitarian
OCCUPATION: Lawyer, public official
OTHER GOVERNMENT POSITIONS: Judge in Ohio Superior Court, 1887-90; U.S. Solicitor General, 1890-92; U.S. Circuit Court Judge, 1892-1900; Governor of the Philippines, 1901-04; Secretary of War, 1904-08 (under T. Roosevelt); Chief Justice of the U.S. Supreme Court, 1921-30
MILITARY SERVICE: None
PRESIDENTIAL SALARY:
DIED: March 8, 1930, in Washington, D.C.
AGE AT DEATH: 72 years
CAUSE OF DEATH: Complications of Heart Disease, High Blood Pressure, and Inflammation of the Bladder
BURIED: Arlington, Virginia

William Howard Taft

27th President of the United States (1909 – 1913)

William Howard Taft was born into a prominent family in Cincinnati, Ohio. His father was a prominent lawyer and judge, and his mother was active in the community. People described Taft as being large for his age and somewhat clumsy, but they also noted his intelligence and dedication to his studies.

Before becoming president, Taft had a distinguished career in law and public service. He served as a judge on the Sixth Circuit Court of Appeals and as Governor-General of the Philippines, where he worked to improve infrastructure and modernize the government. He also served as Secretary of War under President Theodore Roosevelt, where he oversaw the construction of the Panama Canal.

During his presidency, Taft focused on issues such as trust-busting and tariff reform. He continued many of the progressive policies of his predecessor, Theodore Roosevelt, and signed important legislation such as the Mann-Elkins Act, which gave the Interstate Commerce Commission more power to regulate the railroads.

After leaving the presidency, Taft continued to play an important role in public life. He served as a professor of law at Yale University and later became the Chief Justice of the United States Supreme Court, where he helped to expand the power of the federal government and protect individual rights. He was also a strong advocate for world peace and worked to establish the League of Nations.

Overall, William Howard Taft had a remarkable life filled with many accomplishments. He was a respected lawyer, judge, and public servant who worked tirelessly to improve the lives of his fellow citizens. Despite facing some challenges during his presidency, he continued to be an important figure in American politics and a champion of progressive values throughout his life.

Fun Facts:

- President Taft threw the first pitch at the opening game of the Washington Senators' season on April 14, 1910.
- He suffered from sleep apnea and often fell asleep during meetings and events.
- He was a prolific letter writer. Taft wrote over 3,000 letters to his wife and children during his presidency alone.
- Taft served as both President of the United States and Chief Justice of the Supreme Court. He is the only person to have held both positions.
- He collected books and reportedly had one of the largest personal libraries of any president. Taft even had a custom-built bookcase installed in the Oval Office.
- He had a pet cow named Pauline Wayne that grazed on the White House lawn and provided milk for the Taft family.
- Taft's family maintained a long-standing political dynasty. His son, Robert (also known as "Mr. Republican"), became a U.S. senator from Ohio and later served as Senate majority leader.
- He was the last president to have facial hair while in office.
- His White House bathtub could fit four men.
- During his tenure at Yale, Taft showed his prowess as a wrestler and achieved the distinction of being Yale's inaugural intramural heavyweight wrestling champion.

Woodrow Wilson (signature)

NICKNAME: "Schoolmaster in Politics," "The Professor," "The Phrasemaker," and "The Father of the League of Nations"
BORN: December 28, 1856, in Staunton, Virginia
POLITICAL PARTY: Democratic
TERM OF OFFICE: March 4, 1913 – March 4, 1921
VICE PRESIDENT: Thomas R. Marshall
AGE AT INAUGURATION: 56 years
NUMBER OF TERMS: Two full terms
PARENTS:
Joseph Ruggles Wilson
Jessie Janet Woodrow Wilson
MARRIED: Ellen Louise Axson Wilson (1860-1914), on June 24, 1885; Edith Bolling Galt Wilson (1872-1961), on December 18 , 1915
CHILDREN: Margaret, Jessie, Eleanor
PETS: Davie the Airedale Terrier and Bruce the Bull Terrier (dogs); Puffins and Mittens the cats, Old Ike the tobacco-chewing ram, songbirds, and 48 sheep (the sheep helped conserve resources during World War I by mowing the White House lawn and the wool was auctioned to raise funds for the American Red Cross)
EDUCATION: Graduated from the College of New Jersey (now Princeton University) (1879)
RELIGION: Presbyterian
OCCUPATION: Teacher, public official
OTHER GOVERNMENT POSITIONS: Governor of New Jersey, 1911-13
MILITARY SERVICE: None
PRESIDENTIAL SALARY: $75,000/year
DIED: February 3, 1924, in Washington, D.C.
AGE AT DEATH: 67 years
CAUSE OF DEATH: Stroke
BURIED: Washington, D.C.

Woodrow Wilson

28th President of the United States (1913 – 1921)

Woodrow Wilson was born in Virginia and raised in the South during the Civil War. His father was a Presbyterian minister, and they brought Wilson up in a deeply religious household. From a young age, he was an excellent student and showed a keen interest in politics and public speaking.

As a young man, Wilson attended Princeton University, where he excelled in academics and became interested in politics. After graduation, he studied law at the University of Virginia, but he eventually turned to academia and became a professor of political science at Princeton. He wrote several books on government and politics, and his work was highly respected in academic circles.

During his presidency, Wilson achieved many significant accomplishments, including the establishment of the Federal Reserve System and the creation of the Federal Trade Commission to regulate business practices. He also signed the Clayton Antitrust Act, which aimed to prevent monopolies and promote competition in the marketplace. Wilson's administration oversaw the implementation of the 19th Amendment to the Constitution, which gave women the right to vote.

His efforts to promote peace and democracy in the world also marked Wilson's presidency. Wilson led the United States into World War I and played a crucial role in negotiating the Treaty of Versailles, which ended the war and established the League of Nations. Wilson received the Nobel Peace Prize in 1919 for his efforts to promote international peace and cooperation.

After leaving office, Wilson remained active in politics and continued to advocate for progressive causes. He suffered a stroke in 1919, which left him partially paralyzed and unable to complete his term as president. Despite his health problems, Wilson remained engaged in public life and wrote extensively on government and politics until his death in 1924.

In summary, Woodrow Wilson was a highly accomplished individual who excelled in academics, politics, and public service. He achieved significant accomplishments during his presidency, including the establishment of important regulatory bodies and the promotion of peace and democracy on the world stage. After leaving office, Wilson remained committed to progressive causes and continued to influence public discourse on government and politics.

Fun Facts:

- Wilson's favorite food was chicken salad, and he is said to have eaten it almost every day for lunch.
- He was the first President to hold regular press conferences with reporters in the White House.
- He kept sheep on the White House lawn to aid the war effort by cutting the grass, and their wool was auctioned to support the American Red Cross.
- Wilson was an avid golfer and played over 1,000 rounds during his presidency.
- Wilson's face is on the $100,000 bill, which was used only for transactions between Federal Reserve Banks and was not circulated among the general public.
- He was the first President of the United States to earn a Ph.D. degree.

Warren G. Harding (signature)

NICKNAME: "President Hardly," "Wobbly Warren," "The Ohio Gang," "Nanook," "Jazz Age President," and "The Poker President"
BORN: November 2, 1865, near Corsica (now Blooming Grove), Ohio
POLITICAL PARTY: Republican
TERM OF OFFICE: March 4, 1921 – August 2, 1923
VICE PRESIDENT: Calvin Coolidge
AGE AT INAUGURATION: 55 years
NUMBER OF TERMS: Died 2 years, 4 months, and 29 days into term
PARENTS:
George Tyron Harding
Phoebe Elizabeth Dickerson Harding
MARRIED: Florence Kling Harding (1860-1924), on July 8, 1891
CHILDREN: With Florence Kling Harding: Marshall (stepchild); with Ann Britton: Elizabeth
PETS: Laddie Boy the Airedale Terrier and Old Boy the Bulldog , Bob and Petey the canaries, and Pete the squirrel who attended press conferences and news briefings
EDUCATION: Graduated from Ohio Central College (1882)
RELIGION: Baptist
OCCUPATION: Journalist, editor-publisher, author, farmer, public official
OTHER GOVERNMENT POSITIONS: Member of Ohio State Senate, 1900-04; Lieutenant-Governor of Ohio, 1904-06; U.S. Senator, 1915-21
MILITARY SERVICE: None
PRESIDENTIAL SALARY: $75,000/year
DIED: August 2, 1923, in San Francisco, California
AGE AT DEATH: 57 years
CAUSE OF DEATH: Heart Attack
BURIED: Marion, Ohio

Warren G. Harding

29th President of the United States (1921 – 1923)

Warren G. Harding was born in the mid-19th century in rural Ohio. He grew up in a poor family and had to work from a young age to help support his family. Despite his difficult upbringing, Harding was a gifted student and excelled in his studies.

Before his presidency, Harding was a successful newspaper editor and publisher, and he also served as a state senator and lieutenant governor in Ohio. He was known for his support of progressive policies, such as women's suffrage and civil rights.

During his presidency, Harding oversaw several significant accomplishments, including the signing of the Fordney-McCumber Tariff Act, which raised tariffs on imported goods in an attempt to protect American businesses. He also signed the Budget and Accounting Act of 1921, which created a more centralized and efficient system of federal budgeting.

Scandals plagued Harding's presidency. Members of Harding's administration accepted bribes in exchange for granting oil drilling rights on public land in the Teapot Dome scandal. The scandal tarnished Harding's legacy and led to a loss of public trust in government.

Despite the scandals that marred his presidency, Harding is remembered as a charismatic and well-liked leader who worked to promote American prosperity and progress.

Fun Facts:

- Harding was an excellent poker player, and he often played high-stakes games with his friends, including some of the wealthiest men in the country.
- He once lost the White House china in a poker game, and Harding had to replace it out of his own pocket.
- His wife Florence Mabel Kling DeWolfe was born to wealth and at the time of their marriage was one of the wealthiest women in Ohio.
- He had an affair with a woman named Nan Britton, who later wrote a book claiming that Harding was the father of her child. DNA testing in 2015 confirmed that Harding was indeed the father.
- Harding died suddenly while on a trip to the West Coast in 1923, and many rumors have circulated about the cause of his death. Some have suggested that he was poisoned, while others believe he died of a heart attack or stroke.
- After his death, Harding's wife burned many of his personal papers, including his letters to his mistress, to protect his reputation.
- Harding had a pet canary named Bob that he kept in his White House office.
- He was the first U.S. president to visit Alaska while in office.
- Harding gave his beloved pet dog, Laddie Boy, great affection and special privileges. During Cabinet meetings, Laddie Boy was provided with his own hand-carved chair to sit on. The White House hosted birthday celebrations for Laddie Boy, inviting other dogs from the neighborhood to join the festivities and serving them dog biscuit cake.
- He was a Freemason and served as the Grand Master of the Masonic Grand Lodge of Ohio.
- His administration was known for its "return to normalcy" campaign, which aimed to restore order and stability after World War I.

Calvin Coolidge

30th President of the United States (1923 – 1929)

NICKNAME: "Silent Cal," "Cautious Cal," and "Cool Cal"
BORN: July 4, 1872, in Plymouth, Vermont
POLITICAL PARTY: Republican
TERM OF OFFICE: August 2, 1923 – March 4, 1929
VICE PRESIDENT: Charles G. Dawes
AGE AT INAUGURATION: 51 years
NUMBER OF TERMS: One partial term (1 year, 7 months, and 2 days), followed by one full term
PARENTS:
John Calvin Coolidge
Victoria Josephine Moor Coolidge
MARRIED: Grace Anna Goodhue Coolidge (1879-1957), on October 4, 1905
CHILDREN: John, Calvin Jr.
PETS: 13 dogs, 2 cats, 6 birds, a pygmy hippo, donkey, 2 raccoons, bobcat, 2 lion cubs, wallaby, and a black bear
EDUCATION: Attended Black River Academy; Graduated from Amherst College (1895)
RELIGION: Congregationalist
OCCUPATION: Lawyer, public official
OTHER GOVERNMENT POSITIONS: Northampton, MA City Councilman, 1899; City Solicitor, 1900-01; Clerk of Courts, 1904; Member of Massachusetts Legislature, 1907-08; Mayor of Northampton, MA, 1910-11; Member of Massachusetts Legislature, 1912-15; Lieutenant-Governor of Massachusetts, 1916-18; Governor of Massachusetts, 1919-20; Vice President, 1921-23 (under Harding)
MILITARY SERVICE: None
PRESIDENTIAL SALARY:
DIED: January 5, 1933, in Northampton, Massachusetts
AGE AT DEATH: 60 years
CAUSE OF DEATH: Coronary Thrombosis
BURIED: Plymouth Notch, Vermont

Calvin Coolidge was born in Vermont, and he grew up on his family's farm. Hard work and a focus on education marked his childhood. He attended Amherst College and graduated with honors in 1895. After college, Coolidge studied law and began practicing in Northampton, Massachusetts. People quickly recognized Calvin Coolidge as a skilled lawyer and elected him to the city council.

Coolidge's political career began in earnest in 1907, when he was elected to the Massachusetts House of Representatives. He quickly gained a reputation as a principled and effective legislator, and in 1912 he was elected to the state senate. He served two terms in the senate and was elected president of that body in 1914.

In 1918, Coolidge was elected lieutenant governor of Massachusetts, and in 1919 he became governor when the incumbent resigned. As governor, Coolidge gained a reputation as a fiscal conservative and a supporter of small government. He cut taxes and reduced the size of the state government, and he was known for his ability to balance the budget.

Coolidge's presidency, which lasted from 1923 to 1929, was marked by several notable accomplishments. He continued his fiscal conservatism and reduced taxes, which helped stimulate economic growth. He also signed the Immigration Act of 1924, which restricted immigration from certain countries and helped establish quotas for immigrants.

During his presidency, Coolidge also worked to promote civil rights and improve race relations. He spoke out against lynching and appointed African Americans to important government positions. He also signed the Indian Citizenship Act, which granted citizenship to Native Americans.

After his presidency, Coolidge remained active in public life. He wrote a number of books, including an autobiography, and he remained a popular speaker. He also served on a number of boards and commissions, and he was involved in various charitable organizations.

Throughout his life, Coolidge was known for his honesty, integrity, and dedication to public service. He was a man of strong principles who believed in the importance of limited government, individual responsibility, and hard work. His legacy as a leader and a statesman continues to be celebrated today.

Fun Facts:

- Coolidge's nickname was "Silent Cal" because he was known for being a man of few words. He once famously remarked, "I have never been hurt by what I have not said."
- He had a pet raccoon named Rebecca who would often roam the White House. Rebecca was known for getting into mischief and even once escaped from the White House and was found two weeks later.
- Coolidge was the first president to have his inauguration broadcast on the radio.
- He was also a fan of mechanical gadgets and enjoyed tinkering with machines. Coolidge even installed a mechanical horse in the White House to ride three times a day.
- Coolidge's father, a notary public and justice of the peace, administered the oath of office to his son when he became President.

Herbert Hoover (signature)

NICKNAME: "The Great Humanitarian," "The Chief," "The Engineer," "The Master of Emergencies," "Wonder Boy," and "The Forgotten Progressive"
BORN: August 10, 1874, in West Branch, Iowa
POLITICAL PARTY: Republican
TERM OF OFFICE: March 4, 1929 – March 4, 1933
VICE PRESIDENT: Charles Curtis
AGE AT INAUGURATION: 54 years
NUMBER OF TERMS: One full term
PARENTS:
Jesse Clark Hoover
Hulda Randall Minthorn Hoover
MARRIED: Lou Henry Hoover (1875-1944), on February 10, 1899
CHILDREN: Herbert, Allan
PETS: Dogs: King Tut the Belgian shepherd, Pat the German shepherd, Weejie the Norwegian elkhound, Big Ben the English foxhound, Glen the Scottish collie, Yukonan the Siberian husky, Patrick the wolfhound; Sonny the black bear, a Virginia opossum named Billy Possum, and the two alligators that belonged to his son Allen Henry Hoover
EDUCATION: Graduated from Stanford University (1895)
RELIGION: Society of Friends (Quaker)
OCCUPATION: Engineer, public official
OTHER GOVERNMENT POSITIONS: Secretary of Commerce, 1921-23 (under Harding); Secretary of Commerce, 1923-28 (under Coolidge)
MILITARY SERVICE: None
PRESIDENTIAL SALARY: $75,000/year
DIED: October 20, 1964, in New York, New York
AGE AT DEATH: 90 years
CAUSE OF DEATH: Cancer
BURIED: West Branch, Iowa

Herbert Hoover

31st President of the United States (1929 – 1933)

Herbert Hoover was born into a Quaker family in Iowa and was orphaned at nine years old. Despite his difficult childhood, he excelled academically and attended Stanford University, where he studied geology and engineering.

Before becoming president, Hoover had a successful career as a mining engineer and businessman. He traveled extensively around the world and was involved in various humanitarian efforts. During World War I, he played a key role in organizing relief efforts for the people of Belgium.

As president, Hoover faced many challenges including the Great Depression. He implemented various policies aimed at stabilizing the economy, including the creation of the Reconstruction Finance Corporation which provided loans to struggling businesses.

Hoover also focused on international affairs during his presidency. He signed the Kellogg-Briand Pact, which renounced war to resolve international disputes. He also advocated for disarmament and worked to strengthen relations between the United States and Latin America.

After leaving office, Hoover continued to be involved in public service. He served as the head of the Hoover Commission, which aimed to improve the efficiency of the federal government. He also led various humanitarian efforts, including the Hoover Institution, which focused on researching and promoting individual freedom and private enterprise.

Overall, Herbert Hoover's life was marked by his successful career as a mining engineer and businessman, his efforts to aid those in need during World War I, his presidency during the Great Depression and his subsequent involvement in public service and humanitarian efforts.

Fun Facts:

- Hoover was the first president born west of the Mississippi River.
- Hoover was an orphan by the age of nine, after his parents died from illness. He was sent to live with relatives in Oregon.
- He was fluent in Mandarin Chinese and spent years as a mining engineer in China, even translating a Chinese mining book to English.
- Hoover skipped high school but studied bookkeeping, typing, and math at a night school. Despite failing most entrance exams, he entered Stanford University in 1891 and graduated with a geology degree, becoming a mining engineer.
- He and his wife, Lou Henry Hoover, were both accomplished outdoors enthusiasts. They frequently went on camping and fishing trips together.
- He was an animal lover, and his pets included a pair of alligators that were gifted to him by an American consul in China. Hoover also had a pet opossum that he named Billy Possum.
- His campaign slogan for the 1928 presidential election was "A chicken in every pot and a car in every garage."
- Hoover became a millionaire by the age of 40 through his work in the mining industry.
- As Secretary of Commerce, he helped to advance air travel's early development, fostering private industry with government support.

CHAPTER 5

NEW DEAL COALITION (1932–1968)

The New Deal Coalition was a political alliance formed in the United States in the 1930s, during the presidency of Franklin D. Roosevelt, and lasted until the late 1960s. The coalition brought together a diverse range of groups, including labor unions, African Americans, Catholics, Jews, and Southern whites, to support the Democratic Party's policies and candidates.

Here is a detailed description and chronology of events within each era of the New Deal Coalition:
1932-1945: The New Deal Era

• 1932: Franklin D. Roosevelt is elected President of the United States. He promises to use the power of the federal government to combat the Great Depression and enact a series of social and economic reforms collectively known as the New Deal.
• 1933: The first hundred days of the Roosevelt administration sees the passage of a flurry of legislation, including the Emergency Banking Act, the Civilian Conservation Corps, the Agricultural Adjustment Act, the National Industrial Recovery Act, and the Tennessee Valley Authority. These programs aimed to stabilize the economy, provide relief to the unemployed, and modernize the nation's infrastructure.
• 1935: Congress passes the Social Security Act, which establishes a system of old-age pensions, unemployment insurance, and welfare benefits for the poor. Other notable legislation includes the National Labor Relations Act, which guarantees workers the right to form unions and bargain collectively, and the Works Progress Administration, which creates jobs for millions of unemployed Americans.
• 1936: Roosevelt is re-elected in a landslide victory over Republican nominee Alf Landon. The Democrats win large majorities in both houses of Congress, cementing their dominance of American politics.
• 1941: The United States enters World War II after the Japanese attack on Pearl Harbor. Roosevelt mobilizes the country for war, and the New Deal's economic policies shift towards full employment and industrial production.

1945-1960: The Postwar Era

• 1945: World War II ends with the defeat of Germany and Japan. Vice President Harry S. Truman succeeded Roosevelt upon his death in office.
• 1946: The Republicans win control of Congress for the first time since 1928. A conservative Congress opposed Truman's efforts to continue the New Deal's domestic policies.
• 1948: Truman wins a surprise victory over Republican nominee Thomas Dewey, thanks in part to support from labor unions and African American voters. He begins a series of civil rights initiatives, including the desegregation of the armed forces.

• 1950s: The New Deal coalition begins to unravel as demographic, social, and economic changes challenge the traditional Democratic Party. The growth of the suburbs, the rise of the middle class, and the decline of manufacturing jobs weaken the labor movement and shift political power to the Sun Belt states.
• 1960: John F. Kennedy is elected President, promising to continue the New Deal's legacy of progress and reform.
1960-1968: The Great Society Era
• 1963: Kennedy is assassinated and is succeeded by Vice President Lyndon B. Johnson. Johnson declares a "War on Poverty" and enacts a series of ambitious social programs collectively known as the Great Society. These include the Civil Rights Act of 1964, the Voting Rights Act of 1965, and the creation of Medicare and Medicaid.
• 1964: Johnson wins a landslide victory over Republican nominee Barry Goldwater. The Democrats expand their majorities in Congress, but the conservative backlash against the Great Society builds.
• 1968: The New Deal coalition finally collapses in the wake of the Vietnam War, civil rights protests, and the urban riots of the late 1960s. Johnson declines to run for re-election, and the Democratic Party.

Franklin D. Roosevelt

32nd President of the United States (1933 – 1945)

NICKNAME: "FDR," "Teddy," "The New Deal President," "The War President," "The Great Communicator," "The Crip," "The Sphinx," and "The Man Who Saved America"
BORN: January 30, 1882, in Hyde Park, New York
POLITICAL PARTY: Democratic
TERM OF OFFICE: March 4, 1933 – April 12, 1945
VICE PRESIDENT: John Nance Garner (1933–1941), Henry A. Wallace (1941–1945), Harry S. Truman (1945)
AGE AT INAUGURATION: 51 years
NUMBER OF TERMS: Three full terms; died 2 months and 23 days into fourth term
PARENTS:
James Roosevelt
Sara Delano Roosevelt
MARRIED: Anna Eleanor Roosevelt (1884-1962), on March 17, 1905
CHILDREN: Anna, James, Franklin Jr., Elliott, Franklin Jr. II, John
PETS: Major (German shepherd), Meggie and Fala (Scottish terriers); President (Great Dane); Tiny (Old English sheepdog); Winks (Llewellyn setter); and Blaze (English bullmastiff)
EDUCATION: Graduated from Harvard College (1903); Attended Columbia Law School
RELIGION: Episcopalian
OCCUPATION: Lawyer, public official
OTHER GOVERNMENT POSITIONS: Member of New York State Legislature, 1911-13; Assistant Secretary of the Navy, 1913-20; Governor of New York, 1929-33
MILITARY SERVICE: None
PRESIDENTIAL SALARY: $75,000/year
DIED: April 12, 1945, in Warm Springs, Georgia
AGE AT DEATH: 63 years
CAUSE OF DEATH: Stroke
BURIED: Hyde Park, New York

Franklin D. Roosevelt is one of the most significant presidents in American history because of his leadership during some of the country's most difficult times. Roosevelt was born into a wealthy family and attended Harvard University, where he became interested in politics. He started his career as a lawyer and quickly became involved in New York state politics.

In 1921, Roosevelt was stricken with polio, which left him paralyzed from the waist down. However, he refused to let his disability hinder his political career, and he became governor of New York in 1928. As governor, Roosevelt implemented a range of progressive policies, such as social welfare programs and labor protections.

Roosevelt was elected president in 1932, during the height of the Great Depression. He launched the New Deal, a series of policies aimed at stimulating economic growth and providing relief for the millions of Americans who were struggling. The New Deal included programs like the Civilian Conservation Corps, which employed young men to work on environmental projects, and the Social Security Act, which provided a safety net for elderly and disabled Americans.

During World War II, Roosevelt led the country through some of its darkest days. He worked with allies to defeat Nazi Germany and played a pivotal role in the formation of the United Nations. Roosevelt was elected to an unprecedented fourth term as president in 1944, but he died just a few months later, before the end of the war. His leadership and legacy continue to shape American politics and society to this day.

Fun Facts:

- Polio paralyzed Roosevelt from the waist down in 1921. He used a wheelchair for the rest of his life and often kept his disability hidden from the public.
- Despite his physical limitations, he remained active throughout his life and enjoyed swimming and sailing.
- He founded the National Foundation for Infantile Paralysis (later known as the March of Dimes) in 1938 to combat polio.
- He was the first president to fly on official business while in office, traveling by airplane in 1943 to a Casablanca conference during WWII.
- Roosevelt tried to change the Supreme Court: In 1937, he proposed a plan to "pack" the Supreme Court by appointing up to six additional justices. Critics widely denounced the plan, and it ultimately failed, but it remains a notable moment in US political history.
- He was known for his love of hot dogs and would often serve them to guests at the White House.
- He was the fifth cousin of Theodore Roosevelt, the 26th president. FDR was found to have distant familial ties to 11 U.S. presidents, including 5 by blood and 6 by marriage. These presidents are John Adams, John Quincy Adams, Ulysses Grant, William Henry Harrison, Benjamin Harrison, James Madison, Theodore Roosevelt, William Taft, Zachary Taylor, Martin Van Buren, and George Washington.
- FDR's superior communication skills shaped American history through speeches, press conferences, and radio broadcasts.

Harry S. Truman

NICKNAME: "Give 'Em Hell Harry" and "The Haberdasher President
BORN: May 8, 1884, in Lamar, Missouri
POLITICAL PARTY: Democratic
TERM OF OFFICE: April 12, 1945 – January 20, 1953
VICE PRESIDENT: Alben W. Barkley
AGE AT INAUGURATION: 60 years
NUMBER OF TERMS: One partial term (3 years, 9 months, and 8 days), followed by one full term
PARENTS:
John Anderson Truman
Martha Ellen Young Truman
MARRIED: Elizabeth "Bess" Virginia Wallace Truman (1885-1982), on June 28, 1919
CHILDREN: Margaret
PETS: Feller the cocker spaniel and Mike, an Irish setter
EDUCATION: Attended the University of Kansas City Law School
RELIGION: Baptist
OCCUPATION: Farmer, public official
OTHER GOVERNMENT POSITIONS: Judge on Jackson County Court, 1922-24; Presiding Judge of Jackson County Court, 1926-34; U.S. Senator, 1935-45; Vice President, 1945 (under FDR)
MILITARY SERVICE: Corporal, Missouri National Guard (1905-1911); Captain, U.S. Army (1917-1919); Colonel, U.S. Army Reserve (1920-1953)
PRESIDENTIAL SALARY: $75,000/year (increased to $100,000 + $50,000 expense account in 1949)
DIED: December 26, 1972, in Kansas City, Missouri
AGE AT DEATH: 88 years
CAUSE OF DEATH: Minor lung congestion, organ failures, cardiovascular system collapse, hypotension, pneumonia
BURIED: Independence, Missouri

Harry S. Truman

33rd President of the United States (1945 – 1953)

Harry S. Truman was a man of humble beginnings who grew up in Independence, Missouri. He was raised on a farm and had to work hard to make a living. Truman served in the National Guard during World War I and later opened a men's clothing store in downtown Kansas City.

Truman launched his political career in the 1920s by being elected as a judge in Jackson County, Missouri. He later served as a United States Senator from Missouri, where he gained a reputation for being tough on corruption and a champion of civil rights.

In 1944, Truman was chosen to be the running mate of President Franklin D. Roosevelt for his fourth term in office. When Roosevelt died in 1945, Truman became the 33rd President of the United States. During his presidency, Truman oversaw the end of World War II, including the use of atomic bombs on Japan. He also played a key role in creating the United Nations, the Marshall Plan, and the Truman Doctrine, which established the U.S. policy of containing Soviet expansion.

Truman faced many challenges during his presidency, including strikes and labor unrest, civil rights issues, and the Korean War. Despite these challenges, Truman remained committed to his principles and worked tirelessly to improve the lives of ordinary Americans.

After leaving office, Truman returned to his hometown of Independence, Missouri, where he lived a quiet life with his wife, Bess. He remained active in public life, however, and continued to speak out on issues he cared about until his death. Truman is remembered as a president who led the United States through a difficult period in its history and who fought tirelessly for the principles of democracy and human rights.

Fun Facts:

- Truman was the last U.S. president who did not have a college degree.
- He was known for his plain-spoken, no-nonsense style.
- Truman was known for his thick glasses, which he started wearing at eight years old. He had poor eyesight, and his glasses were a distinctive part of his appearance.
- He was a passionate poker player who coined the popular phrase, "If you can't stand the heat, get out of the kitchen."
- He was the only president to authorize the use of nuclear weapons, dropping atomic bombs on Hiroshima and Nagasaki in 1945.
- Truman ran a men's clothing store in Kansas City but it struggled, almost bankrupting him. He worked hard to pay off the debts and eventually sold the store.
- He was born in Lamar, Missouri, in a house that has since been torn down. The site is now marked with a historical marker.
- He had a sign on his desk that read, "The buck stops here," showing that he took responsibility for all decisions made by his administration.
- Truman lacked a middle name and the "S" was added to honor his grandfathers, Anderson Shipp Truman and Solomon Young.
- He served as a judge of the Jackson County Court in Missouri from 1922 to 1934.

Dwight D. Eisenhower [signature]

NICKNAME: "Ike," "Kansas Cyclone," "The General," "The Chief," "The G.I. General," "Uncle Ike," "The Smiling Eisenhower," "The Grand Old Man," "The Preacher President," "The Suez Warrior," and "The Highway President"
BORN: October 14, 1890, in Denison, Texas
POLITICAL PARTY: Republican
TERM OF OFFICE: January 20, 1953 – January 20, 1961
VICE PRESIDENT: Richard Milhous Nixon
AGE AT INAUGURATION: 62 years
NUMBER OF TERMS: Two full terms
PARENTS:
David Jacob Eisenhower
Ida Elizabeth Stover Eisenhower
MARRIED: Mary "Mamie" Geneva Doud Eisenhower (1896-1979), on July 1, 1916
CHILDREN: John, Doud
PETS: Dogs: two Scottish Terriers named Caacie and Telek, and a Weimaraner named Heidi; a parakeet named Gabby
EDUCATION: Graduated from U.S. Military Academy, West Point, N.Y. (1915)
RELIGION: Presbyterian
OCCUPATION: Soldier
OTHER GOVERNMENT POSITIONS: None
MILITARY SERVICE: General of the Army, U.S. Army (1915-1948, 1951-1952)
PRESIDENTIAL SALARY: $100,000/year + $50,000 expense account
DIED: March 28, 1969, in Washington, D.C.
AGE AT DEATH: 78 years
CAUSE OF DEATH: Congestive Heart Failure
BURIED: Abilene, Kansas

Dwight D. Eisenhower

34th President of the United States (1953 – 1961)

Dwight D. Eisenhower, commonly known as Ike, was a prominent figure in American history. As a child, he was raised in a poor family in Kansas, where he learned the values of hard work, discipline, and determination that would serve him well throughout his life. After graduating from West Point Military Academy, he served in the U.S. Army, rising to the rank of five-star general during World War II.

As a general, Eisenhower played a crucial role in the Allied victory in Europe during World War II, commanding the D-Day invasion and leading the liberation of France. He was known for his strategic planning and ability to work with leaders from various nations and factions, earning him a reputation as a skilled diplomat as well as a military leader.

After the war, Eisenhower served as the Supreme Commander of the Allied Forces in Europe and was appointed as the first Supreme Commander of NATO, where he helped to establish the post-war military alliance between North America and Europe.

In 1952, Eisenhower was elected as the 34th President of the United States. During his presidency, he implemented policies aimed at promoting economic growth and reducing the federal deficit. He also oversaw the construction of the interstate highway system and the desegregation of public schools, which were landmark achievements in American history.

In foreign policy, Eisenhower is best known for his doctrine of "massive retaliation," which emphasized the use of nuclear weapons to deter aggression from foreign powers. He also negotiated the end of the Korean War and played a crucial role in the peaceful resolution of the Suez Crisis.

After leaving office, Eisenhower continued to be a prominent public figure, speaking out on issues such as the dangers of the military-industrial complex and the need for greater cooperation between nations. He was also involved in the founding of several institutions, including the Eisenhower Foundation, which aims to promote peace and international understanding.

Overall, Dwight D. Eisenhower was a highly accomplished military leader, diplomat, and statesman who played a pivotal role in shaping American history during the 20th century.

Fun Facts:

- Eisenhower was a talented painter and completed over 250 oil paintings during his lifetime, many of which were landscapes.
- He was an accomplished poker player.
- He was an avid fan of western movies and often watched them in the White House theater.
- Eisenhower was a chain smoker for much of his life, and would often smoke up to four packs of cigarettes a day.
- Eisenhower suffered a heart attack while in office in 1955, which led to concerns about his health and ability to serve as president.
- Despite being a military general, Eisenhower was not a fan of war and famously warned against the military-industrial complex in his farewell address.

NICKNAME: "JFK" and "Jack"
BORN: May 29, 1917, in Brookline, Massachusetts
POLITICAL PARTY: Democratic
TERM OF OFFICE: January 20, 1961 – November 22, 1963
VICE PRESIDENT: Lyndon Baines Johnson
AGE AT INAUGURATION: 43 years
NUMBER OF TERMS: Assassinated: died 2 years, 10 months, and 2 days into term
PARENTS:
Joseph Patrick Kennedy
Rose Elizabeth Fitzgerald Kennedy
MARRIED: Jacqueline Lee Bouvier Kennedy (1929-1994), on September 12, 1953
CHILDREN: Caroline, John Jr., Patrick
PETS: Tom Kitten the cat; Robin the canary; Zsa Zsa the rabbit; Sardar the horse; ponies named Macaroni, Tex, and Leprechaun; parakeets named Bluebell and Marybelle; hamsters named Debbie and Billie; Charlie, a Welsh terrier, plus dogs named Pushinka, Shannon, and Clipper
EDUCATION: Graduated from Harvard College (1940)
RELIGION: Roman Catholic
OCCUPATION: Author, public official
OTHER GOVERNMENT POSITIONS: Member of U.S. House of Representatives, 1947-53; United States Senator, 1953-61
MILITARY SERVICE: Lieutenant, U.S. Naval Reserve (1941-1945)
PRESIDENTIAL SALARY: $100,000/year + $50,000 expense account (refused by Kennedy)
DIED: November 22, 1963, in Dallas, Texas
AGE AT DEATH: 46 years
CAUSE OF DEATH: Gunshot Wound
BURIED: Arlington, Virginia

John F. Kennedy

35th President of the United States (1961 – 1963)

John F. Kennedy, often referred to as JFK, was an American politician and lawyer who had a remarkable life before becoming the President of the United States. Kennedy was born into a wealthy family and grew up in the affluent area of Brookline, Massachusetts. As a child, he was a sickly boy and suffered from a variety of ailments, including asthma, for which he received medical treatment throughout his life.

During his early years, Kennedy attended several private schools, including the prestigious Choate School in Connecticut. In 1940, he enrolled at Harvard University, where he excelled in academics and athletics. After graduating, Kennedy joined the U.S. Navy and served with distinction during World War II.

In 1946, Kennedy was elected to the U.S. House of Representatives, where he served for six years before being elected to the U.S. Senate in 1952. During his time in Congress, Kennedy was known for his advocacy of civil rights, his support for education and healthcare reform, and his firm stance on foreign policy.

Several significant accomplishments marked Kennedy's presidency, which began in 1961. He established the Peace Corps, a volunteer organization that sends Americans abroad to assist with development projects in other countries. He also launched the Apollo space program, which resulted in the first moon landing in 1969.

Kennedy played a crucial role in the Cuban Missile Crisis, a tense standoff between the U.S. and the Soviet Union that nearly led to nuclear war. Kennedy's leadership during this crisis helped to prevent a catastrophic outcome and earned him widespread praise, both domestically and internationally.

On November 22, 1963, John F. Kennedy was assassinated in Dallas, Texas, ending his presidency prematurely. The assassination remains one of the most significant events in American history and has been the subject of countless investigations, theories, and debates. Kennedy's legacy as a charismatic leader who inspired a generation to public service has endured long after his death.

Fun Facts:

- Kennedy was an accomplished sailor and won the Nantucket Sound Star Class Regatta in 1936.
- He was the first president to hold a press conference on live television.
- He was the first president to be born in the 20th century.
- He suffered from several health problems, including Addison's disease, chronic back pain, and colitis.
- Kennedy won a Pulitzer Prize in 1957 for his book "Profiles in Courage," which he wrote while recovering from back surgery.
- He was a speed reader and was known to read eight newspapers daily.
- He was a fan of James Bond novels, and even met Ian Fleming, the author of the series, in 1960.
- Kennedy was a big fan of the musical "Camelot," and after his death, his widow Jacqueline Kennedy referred to his presidency as "Camelot" in a Life magazine interview.
- His favorite food was New England fish chowder, which he would have served on Fridays in the White House.

Lyndon B. Johnson

36th President of the United States (1963 – 1969)

NICKNAME: "LBJ," "Landslide Lyndon," "Light Bulb Lyndon," and "Rufus Cornpone"
BORN: August 27, 1908, near Johnson City, Texas
POLITICAL PARTY: Democratic
TERM OF OFFICE: November 22, 1963 – January 20, 1969
VICE PRESIDENT: Hubert Horatio Humphrey
AGE AT INAUGURATION: 55 years
NUMBER OF TERMS: One partial term (1 year, 1 month, and 29 days), followed by one full term
PARENTS:
Sam Ealy Johnson, Jr.
Rebekah Baines Johnson
MARRIED: Claudia Alta Taylor "Lady Bird" Johnson (1912-2007), on November 17, 1934
CHILDREN: Lynda, Luci
PETS: Dogs: Blanco the collie, Yuki the mutt, Him, Her, Edgar, and Freckles (all beagles); hamsters and lovebirds
EDUCATION: Graduated from Southwest Texas State Teachers College (1930) (now known as Texas State University-San Marcos)
RELIGION: Disciples of Christ
OCCUPATION: Teacher, public official
OTHER GOVERNMENT POSITIONS:
Congressional Secretary, 1931-37; Member of U.S. House of Representatives, 1937-49; U.S. Senator, 1949-61; Vice President, 1961-63 (under Kennedy)
MILITARY SERVICE: Commander, U.S. Naval Reserve (1940-1964)
PRESIDENTIAL SALARY:
$100,000/year + $50,000 expense account
DIED: January 22, 1973, near Johnson City, Texas
AGE AT DEATH: 64 years
CAUSE OF DEATH: Heart Attack
BURIED: Stonewall, Texas

Lyndon B. Johnson was born into a family of modest means in rural Texas. Poverty and hard work marked his childhood, as his family struggled to make ends meet on their small farm. Despite the challenges he faced, Johnson was a gifted student and attended college at Southwest Texas State Teachers College, where he excelled in debate and public speaking.

Prior to becoming president, Johnson had a long and distinguished career in politics. He served in the U.S. House of Representatives and later in the U.S. Senate, where he became known as a skillful negotiator and dealmaker. Johnson was a key architect of many important pieces of legislation, including the Civil Rights Act of 1957 and the Voting Rights Act of 1965.

As president, Johnson oversaw a period of tremendous social and economic change in the United States. He championed civil rights and signed into law the Civil Rights Act of 1964 and the Voting Rights Act of 1965, which helped to dismantle the legal barriers that had long prevented African Americans from fully participating in American democracy. Johnson also launched a wide range of programs to combat poverty and promote economic growth, including the creation of Medicare and Medicaid.

After leaving office, Johnson continued to be an influential figure in American politics. He worked tirelessly to promote education and served as the founding director of the Lyndon B. Johnson Presidential Library and Museum in Austin, Texas. Johnson also remained active in Democratic Party politics, serving as a key advisor to many prominent political figures.

Lyndon B. Johnson's intelligence, political savvy, and leadership abilities were widely recognized throughout his life. He was a tireless advocate for social justice and economic opportunity, and his legacy continues to shape American politics and society to this day.

Fun Facts:

- Johnson had a pet beagle named Him who often accompanied him to the Oval Office.
- He was notorious for his love of practical jokes and would often play them on his staff and political opponents.
- He was known for his crude language and would often use vulgarities in private conversations, even with foreign leaders.
- Johnson was a fan of Fresca, a grapefruit-flavored soda, and had a button installed in the Oval Office that would summon a White House steward to bring him a can.
- He was a prolific telephone talker and would often make personal calls to friends and associates, sometimes in the middle of the night.
- He had a private bathroom installed in Air Force One, which was equipped with a shower, a hair dryer, and a leather chair.
- Johnson owned an amphibious car that he would often use to surprise and scare his guests by driving straight into a lake or river.
- He was a fan of barbecue and often hosted cookouts at the LBJ Ranch in Texas.
- He quoted Shakespeare and other famous writers.

CHAPTER 6

ERA OF DIVIDED GOVERNMENT (1968–2000)

The Era of Divided Government refers to the period between 1968 and 2000 in the United States, during which different political parties controlled the presidency and Congress for extended periods of time. This era saw several significant political and social events, as well as changes in the political landscape of the country. Here is a chronology of events within each era:

1968-1976:

- Richard Nixon, a Republican, wins the presidential election in 1968, marking the beginning of the Era of Divided Government.
- The Environmental Protection Agency (EPA) was created in 1970 to address the growing concerns over pollution and environmental degradation.
- The Watergate scandal, which began in 1972, eventually leads to Nixon's resignation in 1974.
- Democrat Jimmy Carter won the 1976 presidential election, marking the end of the Nixon-Ford administration and the beginning of a period of unified Democratic control of the government.

1976-1980:

- Congress passed the Foreign Intelligence Surveillance Act (FISA) in 1978, establishing a legal framework for government surveillance activities.
- In 1980, Republican Ronald Reagan is elected president, and the Republicans gain control of the Senate, marking the beginning of a period of divided government.

1980-1992:

- Reagan's presidency is marked by a focus on deregulation and tax cuts, as well as an increase in defense spending and military intervention abroad.
- In 1986, the Immigration Reform and Control Act is passed, which grants amnesty to undocumented immigrants already living in the United States and establishes penalties for employers who knowingly hire undocumented workers.
- Democrat Bill Clinton, who campaigns on a platform of economic reform and social justice won the 1992 presidential election.

1992-2000:

- Clinton's presidency is marked by a focus on welfare reform, gun control, and healthcare reform.
- In 1994, Republicans gain control of both the House and Senate for the first time in 40 years, leading to a period of divided government.
- The 1998 impeachment of Clinton, stemming from a scandal involving a sexual relationship with a White House intern, ends with Clinton's acquittal by the Senate.
- Republican George W. Bush won the 2000 presidential election, marking the end of the Era of Divided Government.

During the Era of Divided Government, notable events included the end of the Cold War, Gulf War, 9/11, and the dot-com boom and bust, all amidst significant political polarization between major parties vying for control.

Richard Nixon (signature)

NICKNAME: "Gloomy Gus," "Tricky Dick," and "Tricky Dicky"
BORN: January 9, 1913, in Yorba Linda, California
POLITICAL PARTY: Republican
TERM OF OFFICE: January 20, 1969 – August 9, 1974
VICE PRESIDENT: Spiro T. Agnew (1969–1973), Gerald Rudolph Ford (1973–1974)
AGE AT INAUGURATION: 56 years
NUMBER OF TERMS: One full term; resigned 1 year, 6 months, and 20 days into second term
PARENTS:
Francis Anthony Nixon
Hannah Milhous Nixon
MARRIED: Patricia Ryan Nixon (1912-1993), on June 21, 1940
CHILDREN: Patricia, Julie.
PETS: Checkers the cocker spaniel, Vicky the poodle, Pasha the terrier, King Timahoe the Irish setter, and fish
EDUCATION: Graduated from Whittier College (1934) and Duke University Law School (1937)
RELIGION: Society of Friends (Quaker)
OCCUPATION: Lawyer, public official
OTHER GOVERNMENT POSITIONS: Attorney for U.S. Office of Emergency Management, 1942; Member of U.S. House of Representatives, 1947-51; U.S. Senator, 1951-53; Vice President, 1953-61 (under Eisenhower)
MILITARY SERVICE: Commander, U.S. Naval Reserve (1942-1966)
PRESIDENTIAL SALARY: $200,000/year + $50,000 expense account
DIED: April 22, 1994, in New York, New York
AGE AT DEATH: 81 years
CAUSE OF DEATH: Stroke
BURIED: Yorba Linda, California

Richard Nixon

37th President of the United States (1969 – 1974)

Richard Nixon was born in Yorba Linda, California, in 1913. As a child, he worked hard and was an excellent student, excelling in debate and drama in high school. He attended Whittier College, where he continued to excel academically and became involved in student politics.

After college, Nixon attended Duke University Law School and graduated in 1937. He then returned to California and began practicing law, eventually joining the Navy during World War II. After the war, Nixon ran for Congress and was elected to the House of Representatives in 1946. During his time in Congress, Nixon became well known for his aggressive questioning of witnesses during the investigation of Alger Hiss, a government official accused of spying for the Soviet Union.

In 1950, Nixon ran for the Senate and won, becoming a prominent figure in the Republican Party. In 1952, he was selected as Dwight D. Eisenhower's running mate in the presidential election and served as Vice President from 1953 to 1961.

During his presidency, Nixon was known for his efforts to improve relations with China and the Soviet Union, which were both seen as significant achievements. He also implemented policies, such as the creation of the Environmental Protection Agency and the Occupational Safety and Health Administration.

The Watergate scandal ultimately forced Nixon to resign in 1974, marking his presidency with controversy. Despite this setback, Nixon continued to be active in public life after leaving office, writing several books and making public appearances. He also played a significant role in the normalization of relations between the United States and China, traveling to the country several times and meeting with Chinese leaders.

In summary, Richard Nixon was a highly accomplished individual who rose to prominence through hard work and dedication. He achieved many notable accomplishments throughout his career, including his efforts to improve international relations and his work to protect the environment. Despite his accomplishments, Richard Nixon resigned from the presidency in the wake of the Watergate scandal. Despite this setback, Nixon continued to be active in public life after leaving office, and his legacy continues to be studied and debated today.

Fun Facts:

- Nixon was a talented pianist and reportedly considered pursuing a career as a musician before entering politics.
- He was an avid bowler and even installed a one-lane bowling alley in the basement of the White House.
- He enjoyed ketchup on cottage cheese, a food combination that many people find unusual.
- Nixon had a pet dog named Checkers, which he famously mentioned in a 1952 speech to defend himself against accusations of financial impropriety.
- He was the first president to visit all 50 states while in office.
- Nixon was a big fan of the movie Patton, and he watched it several times while in the White House.
- He had a secret White House taping system, which ultimately led to his downfall during the Watergate scandal.

Gerald R. Ford

NICKNAME: "Jerry" and "Mr. Nice Guy"
BORN: July 14, 1913, in Omaha, Nebraska
POLITICAL PARTY: Republican
TERM OF OFFICE: August 9, 1974 – January 20, 1977
VICE PRESIDENT: Nelson Rockefeller
AGE AT INAUGURATION: 61 years
NUMBER OF TERMS: One partial term (2 years, 5 months, and 11 days
PARENTS:
Leslie Lynch King
Gerald Rudolff Ford (stepfather)
Dorothy Ayer Gardner King Ford
MARRIED: Elizabeth "Betty" Bloomer Warren Ford (1918-2011), on October 15, 1948
CHILDREN: Michael, John, Steven, Susan
PETS: Liberty and Misty the Golden retrievers, Lucky the mixed-breed dog, and Misty Chan the Siamese Cat
EDUCATION: Graduated from the University of Michigan (1935) and Yale University Law School (1941)
RELIGION: Episcopalian
OCCUPATION: Lawyer, public official
OTHER GOVERNMENT POSITIONS: Member of U.S. House of Representatives, 1949-73; Vice President, 1973-74 (under tiny U.S. flag Nixon)
MILITARY SERVICE: Lieutenant Commander, U.S. Naval Reserve (1942-1946)
PRESIDENTIAL SALARY: $200,000/year + $50,000 expense account
DIED: December 26, 2006 in Rancho Mirage, California
AGE AT DEATH: 93 years
CAUSE OF DEATH: Cardiovascular Disease
BURIED: Grand Rapids, Michigan

Gerald Ford

38th President of the United States (1974 – 1977)

Gerald Ford grew up in Grand Rapids, Michigan, where his father worked as a paint salesman. Ford was an athlete in high school and college, playing football for the University of Michigan. After graduating, he attended Yale Law School, where he earned his law degree.

Prior to his presidency, Ford served in the U.S. Navy during World War II and then served in the U.S. House of Representatives for 25 years. During his time in Congress, Ford was known for his work on budgetary issues and his efforts to promote bipartisanship.

As president, Ford faced several challenges, including an economic recession and the fallout from the Watergate scandal. One of his most notable accomplishments was his decision to pardon former President Richard Nixon for his role in the scandal. While controversial many historians now view the pardon as a necessary step to help the country move on from the crisis.

Ford also played a key role in promoting human rights around the world, and his administration helped to negotiate the Helsinki Accords, a series of agreements aimed at improving relations between Western and Eastern Europe.

After leaving office, Ford continued to be active in public life, serving on various boards and foundations. He also established the Gerald R. Ford Presidential Foundation, which supports programs and initiatives related to public service and leadership.

Besides his public service, Ford was also an accomplished athlete and an avid golfer. He was inducted into the Michigan Sports Hall of Fame and the World Golf Hall of Fame, and he continued to play golf well into his 90s.

Fun Facts:

- Ford was born Leslie Lynch King, Jr. in Omaha, Nebraska in 1913. His parents separated just weeks after he was born and his mother later married Gerald R. Ford, Sr., who adopted him and gave him his new name.
- He was never elected as either President or Vice President. Ford became President after Nixon resigned in 1974 but lost to Jimmy Carter in the 1976 election.
- He was a male model in his youth, and even appeared on the cover of Cosmopolitan magazine in 1942.
- He was a skilled athlete and was offered professional football contracts by the Detroit Lions and the Green Bay Packers. However, he turned them down to attend Yale Law School.
- Ford was known for his clumsiness and was frequently involved in accidents. He once accidentally hit a golf ball into the head of a spectator and fell down the stairs of Air Force One.
- In 1975, Ford survived two failed assassination attempts in just 17 days.
- Ford's golden retriever, Liberty, fetched items for him.
- In 1976, Ford pardoned former President Richard Nixon for any crimes he may have committed during his time in office. The decision was controversial and drew criticism from many Americans.
- He was a Distinguished Eagle Scout, the highest Boy Scouts of America honor.

Jimmy Carter (signature)

NICKNAME: "Jimmy," "Peanut Farmer," "The Peanut President," "Mr. Nice Guy," "The Humanitarian President," and "The Malaise President"
BORN: October 1, 1924, in Plains, Georgia
POLITICAL PARTY: Democratic
TERM OF OFFICE: January 20, 1977 – January 20, 1981
VICE PRESIDENT: Walter Mondale
AGE AT INAUGURATION: 52 years
NUMBER OF TERMS: One full term
PARENTS:
James Earl Carter
Lillian Gordy Carter
MARRIED: Eleanor Rosalynn Smith Carter (1928-), on July 7, 1946
CHILDREN: John, James, Donnell, Amy
PETS: Grits the Border collie (mix) dog (Given to his daughter Amy by her teacher, but quickly returned after snapping at several White House visitors), Lewis Brown the Afghan hound dog, and Misty Malarky Ying Yang, daughter Amy Carter's pet Siamese cat
EDUCATION: Attended Georgia Southwestern State University (1942); Attended Georgia Institute of Technology (1943); Graduated from U.S. Naval Academy, Annapolis, Md. (1946)
RELIGION: Baptist
OCCUPATION: Naval officer, farmer, businessman, public official
OTHER GOVERNMENT POSITIONS: Georgia State Senator, 1963-66; Governor of Georgia, 1971-75
MILITARY SERVICE: Lieutenant, U.S. Navy (1946-1953); Lieutenant, U.S. Naval Reserve (1953-1961)
PRESIDENTIAL SALARY: $200,000/year + $50,000 expense account

Jimmy Carter

39th President of the United States (1977 – 1981)

Jimmy Carter was born in Plains, Georgia, and grew up on a farm. As a child, he worked hard, often helping his family with chores like picking cotton and working in the peanut fields. He was a bright student and enjoyed reading, and he was especially interested in history and politics.

After finishing high school, Carter attended Georgia Southwestern College and later transferred to the United States Naval Academy, where he graduated in 1946. He served in the Navy for several years, including on a submarine, before returning to Georgia to take over the family business.

Carter's presidency, which lasted from 1977 to 1981, was marked by several significant accomplishments. One of the most notable was the signing of the Camp David Accords in 1978, which established a peace treaty between Israel and Egypt. He negotiated the SALT II nuclear arms treaty with the Soviet Union, but the U.S. Senate never ratified it.

Domestically, Carter's presidency saw the creation of the Department of Energy and the passage of the National Energy Act, which aimed to reduce dependence on foreign oil. He also signed the Civil Service Reform Act, which aimed to streamline the federal bureaucracy.

After leaving office, Carter continued to be active in public service and advocacy. He founded the Carter Center, a non-profit organization focused on promoting peace and human rights around the world. The Carter Center has been involved in efforts to monitor elections and promote democracy in countries around the world.

Carter has also been active in efforts to eradicate diseases like guinea worm and river blindness in developing countries. His work on these issues has earned him many awards and accolades, including the Nobel Peace Prize in 2002.

Overall, Jimmy Carter's life has been marked by a strong commitment to public service and humanitarian causes. From his early years on the family farm to his post-presidential work on global issues, he has showed a deep compassion for others and a commitment to making the world a better place.

Fun Facts:

- Carter was the first U.S. president to be born in a hospital.
- He is the only president to have reported seeing a UFO.
- A rabbit once attacked Carter while he was fishing. The rabbit was apparently swimming towards his boat and when it got close enough, it attacked the President.
- Carter is a prolific author, having written over 30 books, including memoirs, poetry, and novels.
- He was a peanut farmer before he became a politician, and he continued to manage his family's peanut farm while he was in office.
- Carter was a volunteer with Habitat for Humanity since leaving office, and he helped build houses for the organization into his 90s.
- In 1994, he won a Grammy Award for Best Spoken Word Album for his audiobook version of his autobiography, "Living Faith."
- He was awarded the Nobel Peace Prize in 2002 for his efforts to promote human rights and democracy around the world.

Ronald Reagan (signature)

NICKNAME: "The Gipper," "Dutch," "The Great Communicator," and "Ronnie"
BORN: February 6, 1911, in Tampico, Illinois
POLITICAL PARTY: Republican
TERM OF OFFICE: January 20, 1981 – January 20, 1989
VICE PRESIDENT: George Herbert Walker Bush
AGE AT INAUGURATION: 69 years
NUMBER OF TERMS: Two full terms
PARENTS:
John Edward Reagan
Nelle Wilson Reagan
MARRIED: Jane Wyman (1917-2007), on June 25, 1940 (divorced in 1948); Nancy Davis Reagan (1923-2016), on March 4, 1952
CHILDREN: With first wife Jane Wyman: Maureen, Michael (adopted); with second wife Nancy Davis: Patricia, Ronald
PETS: Lucky the Bouvier des Flandres sheepdog, Rex the Cavalier King Charles spaniel, Victory the golden retriever, Peggy the Irish setter, Taca the Siberian husky, Fuzzy the Belgian sheepdog, and horses
EDUCATION: Graduated from Eureka College (1932)
RELIGION: Disciples of Christ
OCCUPATION: Actor, radio announcer, television host, union leader, public official
OTHER GOVERNMENT POSITIONS: Governor of California, 1967-75
MILITARY SERVICE: Captain, U.S. Army Reserve (1937-1942); Captain, United States Air Forces (1942-1945)
PRESIDENTIAL SALARY: $200,000/year + $50,000 expense account
DIED: June 5, 2004, in Los Angeles, California
AGE AT DEATH: 93 years
CAUSE OF DEATH: Pneumonia
BURIED: Simi Valley, California

Ronald Reagan

40th President of the United States (1981 – 1989)

Ronald Reagan was an American politician, actor, and union leader who served as the 40th President of the United States. Before his presidency, Reagan had a successful career as an actor in Hollywood and served as the Governor of California from 1967 to 1975.

Reagan was born and raised in Illinois and had a modest childhood. His father worked as a shoe salesman and his mother was a homemaker. Reagan attended Eureka College, where he was a popular student and played football. He graduated in 1932 with a degree in economics and sociology.

During his presidency, Reagan's general accomplishments included promoting conservative economic policies, increasing military spending, and strengthening U.S. foreign policy. One of his most significant accomplishments was his role in ending the Cold War, which was a decades-long political and ideological conflict between the United States and the Soviet Union.

Specific accomplishments during Reagan's presidency include the Tax Reform Act of 1986, which simplified the tax code and lowered tax rates for many Americans. Reagan also signed into law the Immigration Reform and Control Act of 1986, which provided amnesty to undocumented immigrants who had been living in the United States since 1982.

After his presidency, Reagan remained an influential figure in American politics and continued to be an advocate for conservative causes. He also became a prolific author, penning several books, including his memoirs, *An American Life*. In 1994, Reagan was diagnosed with Alzheimer's disease, and he passed away in 2004 at 93.

In conclusion, Ronald Reagan had a varied and accomplished life, from his modest upbringing in Illinois to his successful career as an actor and politician. He was a transformative figure during his presidency, promoting conservative economic policies, strengthening U.S. foreign policy, and helping to end the Cold War. After his presidency, Reagan remained an influential figure and continued to be a passionate advocate for conservative causes until his passing.

Fun Facts:

- Reagan was the first president to have been divorced.
- He was an actor before he entered politics. He appeared in over 50 movies, including the 1940 film *Knute Rockne, All American*, in which he played the role of football player George Gipp.
- In 1981, Reagan was shot by a would-be assassin, John Hinckley Jr. He was hit in the chest and suffered a punctured lung, but he made a full recovery.
- He was known for his love of jelly beans and always had a jar of them on his desk in the Oval Office. He even had a special dispenser installed in his presidential limousine.

Geo Bush

NICKNAME: "Little Pops," "Poppy," "Poppy Bush," "Skin," "Papa Bush," "Bush 41," "Bush Senior," and "Senior"
BORN: June 12, 1924, in Milton, Massachusetts
POLITICAL PARTY: Republican
TERM OF OFFICE: January 20, 1989 – January 20, 1993
VICE PRESIDENT: J. Danforth Quayle
AGE AT INAUGURATION: 64 years
NUMBER OF TERMS: One full term
PARENTS:
Prescott Sheldon Bush
Dorothy Walker Bush
MARRIED: Barbara Pierce Bush (1925-2018), on January 6, 1945
CHILDREN: George, John, Robin, Neil, Marvin, Dorothy
PETS: Millie and Ranger, who are both English Springer Spaniels. Millie had her own book called *Millie's Book: As Dictated to Barbara Bush*
EDUCATION: Graduated from Yale University (1948)
RELIGION: Episcopalian
OCCUPATION: Businessman, public official
OTHER GOVERNMENT POSITIONS: Member of U.S. House of Representatives, 1967-71; U.S. Ambassador to the United Nations, 1971-72; Director of the Central Intelligence Agency, 1976-77; Vice President, 1981-89 (under Reagan)
MILITARY SERVICE: Lieutenant (junior grade), U.S. Navy (1942-1955)
PRESIDENTIAL SALARY: $200,000/year + $50,000 expense account
DIED: November 30, 2018, in Houston, Texas
AGE AT DEATH: 94 years
CAUSE OF DEATH: Parkinson's Disease
BURIED: College Station, Texas

George H. W. Bush

41st President of the United States (1989 – 1993)

George H.W. Bush had a privileged upbringing, born into a wealthy family in Massachusetts. He attended prestigious schools and was a talented athlete in his youth, playing baseball and captaining the tennis team in college.

Before his presidency, Bush had a long and varied career in public service. He served as a naval aviator in World War II, was elected to the House of Representatives in 1966, and later served as the U.S. Ambassador to the United Nations and Director of the Central Intelligence Agency.

During his presidency, Bush is credited with achieving several notable accomplishments. He successfully managed the end of the Cold War and oversaw the peaceful reunification of Germany. He also led the U.S. during the Gulf War, which saw a coalition of nations fight against Iraq's invasion of Kuwait.

In addition to his foreign policy achievements, Bush also signed several important pieces of legislation into law during his presidency. These include the Americans with Disabilities Act and the Clean Air Act Amendments of 1990.

After his presidency, Bush continued to be active in public service and philanthropy. He established the George Bush Presidential Library and Museum in Texas and worked to raise funds for disaster relief efforts, including after Hurricane Katrina and the Indian Ocean tsunami.

Overall, George H.W. Bush had a long and distinguished career in public service, marked by a strong commitment to his country and a dedication to improving the lives of others.

Fun Facts:

- Bush was known for his love of skydiving and celebrated his 75th, 80th, and 85th birthdays by skydiving.
- He was once a CIA director: Before becoming Vice President and eventually President, Bush was the Director of the Central Intelligence Agency from 1976 to 1977.
- He was once the captain of the Yale baseball team.
- He was born with the name "George Herbert Walker Bush": The "H.W." stands for "Herbert Walker."
- Bush was once a pilot in World War II: He was the youngest pilot in the Navy during World War II, and he flew 58 combat missions.
- He was a big proponent of volunteerism: During his presidency, Bush created the Points of Light Foundation, which encouraged volunteerism and recognized individuals and organizations that were making a difference in their communities.
- He hated broccoli: Bush famously declared that he did not like broccoli and would never eat it. In fact, he banned it from Air Force One during his presidency.
- He was married to Barbara Bush for 73 years: Bush and his wife Barbara had one of the longest marriages in presidential history, lasting 73 years until Barbara's death in 2018.
- Bush was once a member of the secret society Skull and Bones at Yale University.
- He wore colorful socks to add a pop of color to his outfits.

Bill Clinton (signature)

NICKNAME: "Bill," "Bubba," "The Comeback Kid," "Slick Willie," "The Big Dog," "Elvis," "The Man from Hope," and "The Secretary of Explaining Stuff,"
BORN: August 19, 1946, in Hope, Arkansas
POLITICAL PARTY: Democratic
TERM OF OFFICE: January 20, 1993 – January 20, 2001
VICE PRESIDENT: Albert Gore, Jr.
AGE AT INAUGURATION: 46 years
NUMBER OF TERMS: Two full terms
PARENTS:
William Jefferson Blythe III
Roger Clinton (stepfather)
Virginia Clinton Cassidy
MARRIED: Hillary Rodham Clinton (1947-), on October 11, 1975
CHILDREN: Chelsea
PETS: Socks the black and white "tuxedo" cat and Buddy the chocolate Labrador retriever. Hillary Clinton's book *Dear Socks, Dear Buddy: Kids' Letters to the First Pets* highlights the significance of letter writing, as demonstrated through the White House mail received by Buddy and Socks. The books explains how letters were processed, read, and replied to at U.S. Soldiers' and Airmen's Home.
EDUCATION: Graduated from Georgetown University (1968); Attended Oxford University (1968-70); Graduated from Yale University Law School (1973)
RELIGION: Baptist
OCCUPATION: Lawyer, public official
OTHER GOVERNMENT POSITIONS: Arkansas Attorney General, 1976-78; Governor of Arkansas, 1978-80, 1982-92
MILITARY SERVICE: None
PRESIDENTIAL SALARY: $200,000/year + $50,000 expense account

Bill Clinton

42nd President of the United States (1993 –2001)

Bill Clinton was born in Hope, Arkansas in 1946. He grew up in a small town and faced many challenges in his childhood. His father died before he was born, and his stepfather was an alcoholic who abused his mother. Despite these difficulties, Clinton excelled academically and showed a strong interest in politics from a young age.

Clinton attended Georgetown University and then studied law at Yale. After graduating, he worked as a law professor and then as the Attorney General of Arkansas. In 1978, he was elected as the state's governor and served two terms. During his time as governor, he made significant improvements to education and healthcare in the state.

In 1992, Clinton was elected as the 42nd President of the United States. During his presidency, he accomplished many things, including signing the Family and Medical Leave Act, which allowed workers to take unpaid leave for family or medical reasons. He also signed the North American Free Trade Agreement, which created a free trade zone between the U.S., Canada, and Mexico.

Clinton is also known for his efforts to balance the federal budget and reduce the national debt. He worked with both Democrats and Republicans to create a budget plan that included spending cuts and tax increases.

Another major accomplishment of Clinton's presidency was the passage of the Violence Against Women Act. This law provided funding for programs to help prevent and respond to domestic violence, sexual assault, and stalking.

After leaving office, Clinton continued to be active in politics and philanthropy. He established the Clinton Foundation, which focuses on global health, economic growth, and environmental sustainability. He also worked with his wife, Hillary Clinton, during her presidential campaigns in 2008 and 2016.

Besides his work in politics, Clinton is also an accomplished author and speaker. He has written several books, including a memoir of his presidency, and is a popular speaker on topics such as leadership and public service.

Overall, Bill Clinton's life has been marked by a commitment to public service and a dedication to improving the lives of others. From his childhood in a small town to his time in the White House and beyond, he has been a leader and a role model for generations of Americans.

Fun Facts:

- Clinton is allergic to both chocolate and gluten.
- Clinton has played the saxophone since he was in high school. He famously performed on The Arsenio Hall Show in 1992, playing "Heartbreak Hotel" and wearing sunglasses.
- He is an avid crossword puzzle enthusiast, regularly solving the Sunday Times puzzle, and whenever possible, tackling the Thursday through Saturday puzzles.
- His favorite food is pizza.
- Clinton adopted a vegan diet in 2010 for health reasons, but he has since incorporated fish and eggs into his diet occasionally.
- He was also involved in the Monica Lewinsky scandal, which led to his impeachment by the House of Representatives in 1998.

CHAPTER 7

ERA OF POLITICAL POLARIZATION (2000–PRESENT)

The Era of Political Polarization (2000-Present) is a period marked by increasingly divided political ideologies and partisanship in the United States. Here is a detailed description and chronology of the major events that have occurred during this era:

The 2000 Presidential Election (2000):

The presidential election of 2000 between Republican candidate George W. Bush and Democratic candidate Al Gore was one of the closest and most controversial elections in U.S. history. The election ultimately ended in a Supreme Court decision, with Bush being declared the winner.

September 11 Attacks (2001):

On September 11, 2001, terrorists affiliated with the extremist group Al-Qaeda hijacked four commercial airplanes and crashed them into the Twin Towers of the World Trade Center in New York City, the Pentagon in Washington D.C., and a field in Pennsylvania. Nearly 3,000 people were killed in the attacks, which led to a global War on Terror.

Iraq War (2003-2011):

In 2003, the United States launched a war against Iraq, citing concerns over the country's alleged possession of weapons of mass destruction and links to terrorism. The war lasted for eight years and cost thousands of lives and trillions of dollars.

Hurricane Katrina (2005):

In August 2005, Hurricane Katrina devastated the city of New Orleans and other areas along the Gulf Coast. Critics widely condemned the government's inadequate response to the disaster, particularly to provide aid to those who were affected by the storm.

Financial Crisis (2008):

The collapse of the housing market and the subprime mortgage industry triggered the financial crisis of 2008, also known as the Great Recession. The crisis led to widespread job losses, bank failures, and a deep economic recession that lasted for years.

Obama Presidency (2009-2017):

In 2008, Barack Obama was elected as the first African American President of the United States. Efforts to reform healthcare, the economy, and immigration policy, as well as major accomplishments marked his presidency such as the passage of the Affordable Care Act (Obamacare) and the legalization of same-sex marriage.

Rise of the Tea Party (2009-2010):

The Tea Party movement emerged in 2009 in response to what many conservative Americans saw as excessive government spending and overreach by the federal government. The movement played a major role in the 2010 midterm elections, helping Republicans take control of the House of Representatives.

Trump Presidency (2017-2021):

In 2016, businessman and reality television personality Donald Trump was elected as the 45th President of the United States. Controversy and division marked his presidency, with policies and rhetoric that often stoked racial and cultural tensions. The Trump administration also faced multiple investigations into alleged ties with Russia and other countries.

Capitol Riot (2021):

On January 6, 2021, supporters of President Donald Trump stormed the U.S. Capitol building to try to overturn the results of the 2020 presidential election. The riot resulted in the deaths of five people and led to the impeachment of Trump for incitement of insurrection.

Overall, a series of significant events that have contributed to a growing divide between political parties and ideologies in the United States have marked the Era of Political Polarization.

George W. Bush

43rd President of the United States (2001 – 2009)

NICKNAME: "Dubya," "W," "GW," "GWB," "Bush Jr." "Bush the Younger," "Baby Bush," "Bush 43," "43," "Bush II," "The Decider," "Shrub," "Bushie," "Uncurious George," Incurious George," "The Smirking Chimp," "The Great Divider," "Dumbya," "King George III"
BORN: July 6, 1946, in New Haven, Connecticut
POLITICAL PARTY: Republican
TERM OF OFFICE: January 20, 2001 – January 20, 2009
VICE PRESIDENT: Richard Cheney
AGE AT INAUGURATION: 54 years
NUMBER OF TERMS: Two full terms
PARENTS:
George Herbert Walker Bush
Barbara Pierce Bush
MARRIED: Laura Welch Bush (1946-), on November 5, 1977
CHILDREN: Barbara, Jenna (twins)
PETS: Miss Beazley and Barney the Scottish terriers, Spot "Spotty" Fetcher the springer spaniel (and offspring of Millie), India "Willie" the cat, and Ofelia the longhorn cow (who lives at Bush's Prairie Chapel Ranch). The Bushes' orange-striped polydactyl cat Ernie was judged too wild for White House life and was sent to live with a family in California.
EDUCATION: Graduated from Yale University (1968); Graduated from Harvard Business School (1975)
RELIGION: Methodist
OCCUPATION: Businessman, public official
OTHER GOVERNMENT POSITIONS: Governor of Texas, 1995-2000
MILITARY SERVICE: First Lieutenant, Texas Air National Guard (1968-1974)
PRESIDENTIAL SALARY: $400,000/year + $50,000 expense account

George W. Bush is a prominent American politician who served as the President of the United States from 2001 to 2009. Before his presidency, Bush had a successful career in business and public service.

Bush was born into a prominent political family in New Haven, Connecticut. He grew up in Texas and attended Yale University, where he earned a degree in history. After graduation, he worked in the oil industry before turning to politics.

Bush's political career began in 1978 when he ran for Congress in Texas's 19th congressional district. He lost the race, but he continued to work in politics, serving as an advisor to his father's presidential campaign in 1980.

During his presidency, Bush faced significant challenges, including the 9/11 terrorist attacks and the wars in Afghanistan and Iraq. He launched a series of initiatives to combat terrorism, including the creation of the Department of Homeland Security and the Patriot Act.

Bush also pursued domestic policies, including education reform with the No Child Left Behind Act, Medicare prescription drug coverage, and tax cuts. He also signed the Americans with Disabilities Act Amendments Act of 2008, which expanded the protections of the Americans with Disabilities Act of 1990.

After leaving office, Bush has continued to work on public service initiatives. He established the George W. Bush Presidential Center in Dallas, Texas, which includes a library, museum, and policy institute. The center focuses on issues such as economic growth, education reform, and global health.

Besides his public service, Bush has also pursued a passion for painting. He has become a prolific artist, with a focus on portraits of world leaders and military veterans.

In conclusion, George W. Bush has had a varied and accomplished life, from his early career in business and politics to his presidency and post-presidential work. He has faced significant challenges and pursued important policies in both domestic and international affairs. His continued public service and artistic pursuits show a commitment to making a positive impact on the world.

Fun Facts:

- Bush is a distant relative of 15 U.S. presidents, including his father George H. W. Bush, and also of Barack Obama, Franklin Pierce, James Garfield, William Howard Taft, Millard Fillmore, Franklin D. Roosevelt, Rutherford B. Hayes, Chester A. Arthur, Ulysses S. Grant, Calvin Coolidge, Grover Cleveland, Richard Nixon, Gerald Ford, and Herbert Hoover.
- He collected over 250 signed baseballs, including one from Mickey Mantle.
- Bush is the only U.S. president to have an MBA degree. He earned his Master of Business Administration from Harvard Business School in 1975.
- Bush gave up alcohol at 40 after a binge that made him realize he had a problem.
- Bush called his ranch in Crawford, Texas, his "western White House."
- Bush was the head cheerleader for his high school's cheer team during his senior year at Phillips Academy. He continued cheering in college at Yale from 1964 to 1968.
- Bush has both the lowest and highest approval ratings ever recorded.

NICKNAME: "Barry," "Barry O'Bomber," "Barry O," "Bama," "No Drama Obama," "The Chosen One," "President O," "Renegade," "Obamessiah," "Bam," "O-Train," "Rock Obama," "Bamster," "44," and "Dad-in-Chief"
BORN: August 4, 1961, in Honolulu, Hawaii
POLITICAL PARTY: Democratic
TERM OF OFFICE: January 20, 2009 – January 20, 2017
VICE PRESIDENT: Joseph Biden
AGE AT INAUGURATION: 47 years
NUMBER OF TERMS: Two full terms
PARENTS:
Barack Hussein Obama, Sr.
Ann Dunham
MARRIED: Michelle Robinson Obama (1964-), on October 18, 199
CHILDREN: Malia, Sasha
PETS: Bo and Sunny, Portuguese water dogs.
EDUCATION: Attended Occidental College; Graduated Columbia University (1983); Graduated from Harvard Law School (1991)
RELIGION: United Church of Christ
OCCUPATION: Community organizer, lawyer, law professor, public official, author, lecturer, philanthropist
OTHER GOVERNMENT POSITIONS: Member of Illinois State Senate, 1996-2004; U.S. Senator, 2005-08
MILITARY SERVICE: None
PRESIDENTIAL SALARY: $400,000/year + $50,000 expense account

Barack Obama

44th President of the United States (2009 – 2017)

Barack Obama was born in Honolulu, Hawaii, in 1961 to Ann Dunham, a white American from Kansas, and Barack Obama Sr., a black Kenyan economist. His mother and her parents raised him primarily after his parents divorced when he was two years old.

Obama attended Punahou School, a private college preparatory school in Honolulu. After graduating from high school, he moved to Los Angeles to attend Occidental College. He transferred to Columbia University in New York City after two years, where he graduated with a degree in political science in 1983.

After graduating from Columbia, Obama worked as a community organizer in Chicago. He then attended Harvard Law School, where he was the first African-American president of the Harvard Law Review. After graduating from Harvard Law School, Obama returned to Chicago to practice law. He also taught constitutional law at the University of Chicago Law School.

In 1996, Obama was elected to the Illinois State Senate. He served in the state senate for eight years, during which he worked on issues such as health care, education, and economic development.

In 2004, Obama was elected to the United States Senate. He served in the Senate for four years, during which he worked on issues such as health care, immigration, and foreign policy.

In 2008, Obama was elected the 44th President of the United States. He was the first African-American to be elected President of the United States. Obama's presidency was marked by several accomplishments, including the passage of the Affordable Care Act, the end of the Iraq War, and the killing of Osama bin Laden.

After leaving office with high approval ratings in 2017, Barack Obama has remained active in public life. He has accomplished several things, including writing a best-selling memoir called "A Promised Land", giving speeches on a variety of topics such as race, climate change, and democracy, and working on various philanthropic initiatives, like the Obama Foundation. The foundation aims to inspire, empower, and connect people to make positive changes in their world.

Fun Facts:

- Obama was the first African-American President of the United States.
- He is left-handed, which is relatively rare, as only about 10% of people are left-handed.
- He played basketball in high school and continued to play as president, even converting the White House tennis court so a full court game of basketball could be played.
- He has read every Harry Potter book.
- Obama's first job was scooping ice cream at Baskin-Robbins.
- He is a lifelong comic book fan who started collecting them as a child.
- Obama's favorite food is chili, and he even had a chili recipe of his own that he used to make for family and friends.
- He was the first African American president of the Harvard Law Review.
- Obama's father was Kenyan, and his mother was American. He spent part of his childhood in Indonesia and has visited several other countries, including Kenya, throughout his life.

Donald Trump

45th President of the United States (2017 – 2021)

NICKNAME: "The Donald," "Teflon Don," "Trumpster," "Trumplethinskin," "Donnie," "Don," "King of Debt," "Mr. Brexit," "The Orange One," and "The Great White Hope"
BORN: June 14, 1946, in New York, New York
POLITICAL PARTY: Republican
TERM OF OFFICE: January 20, 2017 – January 20, 2021
VICE PRESIDENT: Mike Pence
AGE AT INAUGURATION: 70 years
NUMBER OF TERMS: One full term
PARENTS:
Frederick Christ Trump, Sr.
Mary Anne MacLeod Trump
MARRIED: Ivana Zelníčková (1949-), on April 7, 1977 (divorced in1992); Marla Maples (1963-), on December 20, 1993 (divorced in 1999); Melania Trump (1970-), on January 22, 2005
CHILDREN: With first wife Ivana Trump: Donald Jr., Ivanka, Eric; with second wife Marla Maples: Tiffany; with third wife Melania Trump: Barron
PETS: no pets
EDUCATION: Graduated from the Wharton School of the University of Pennsylvania, with a B.S. in economics
RELIGION: Identifies as 'non-denominational Christian', although raised Presbyterian
OCCUPATION: Real Estate Developer, Businessman, Television Personality, Author
OTHER GOVERNMENT POSITIONS: None
MILITARY SERVICE: None
PRESIDENTIAL SALARY: $400,000/year + $50,000 expense account

Donald Trump is a well-known business magnate, television personality, and politician from the United States. His father, Fred Trump, a successful real estate developer, heavily influenced him while he was growing up in Queens, New York City. After graduating from college, Donald Trump joined his father's company and began working on various real estate projects in the New York City area.

Over the years, Trump expanded his business empire and became involved in a wide range of industries, including casinos, hotels, golf courses, and beauty pageants. He gained national prominence in the 1980s and 1990s as a flamboyant and often controversial public figure, known for his lavish lifestyle and brash personality.

In 2004, Trump began hosting the reality TV show "The Apprentice," which became an enormous hit and made him a household name. The show was known for its catchphrase, "You're fired," which Trump would use to eliminate contestants from the competition.

In 2016, Trump announced his candidacy for President of the United States, running as a Republican. Controversy and divisive rhetoric marked his campaign, but he defeated his Democratic opponent, Hillary Clinton, in a surprising upset.

During his time in office, Trump pursued several controversial policies, including a travel ban on citizens from several predominantly Muslim countries, a crackdown on undocumented immigrants, and a withdrawal from the Paris climate agreement. His presidency was also marked by several high-profile controversies, including an ongoing investigation into his campaign's possible collusion with Russia during the 2016 election, and his impeachments by the House of Representatives in 2019 and 2021.

Since leaving office, Trump has continued to be a divisive figure in American politics. He has made many false claims about the 2020 presidential election, which he lost to Joe Biden, and has faced legal problems, including a pending indictment in New York City. Despite this, he remains a popular figure among his supporters and has continued to wield significant influence in the Republican Party.

Fun Facts:

- Trump has a fear of germs and is known to be a germaphobe.
- He is a prolific user of Twitter, with over 88 million followers, and has often made controversial statements through his social media accounts.
- He is a member of the WWE Hall of Fame and has made several appearances in professional wrestling shows over the years.
- He reportedly sleeps only four hours a night, which is much less than the recommended amount of sleep for adults.
- Trump owned a professional football team, the New Jersey Generals of the United States Football League, in the 1980s.
- He once sued comedian Bill Maher for $5 million over a joke Maher made about Trump's parentage, which Trump claimed was defamatory.
- Trump has his own star on the Hollywood Walk of Fame, awarded to him in 2007 for his work on the reality TV show "The Apprentice."
- He is the only president to have been impeached twice by the House of Representatives.

[signature]

NICKNAME: "Uncle Joe," "Sleepy Joe," "Amtrak Joe," "Diamond Joe," "Scranton Joe," "Bidenator," "Joe Cool," "Lunchbox Joe," "Middle Class Joe," and "Dark Brandon"
BORN: November 20, 1942, in Scranton, Pennsylvania
POLITICAL PARTY: Democratic
TERM OF OFFICE: January 20, 2021 – Present
VICE PRESIDENT: Kamala Harris
AGE AT INAUGURATION: 78 years
NUMBER OF TERMS: Currently serving
PARENTS:
Joseph Robinette Biden, Sr.
Catherine Eugenia "Jean" Biden
MARRIED: Jill Tracy Biden (1951-), on June 17, 1977; Neilia Hunter Biden (1942-72), on August 27, 1966
CHILDREN: With first wife Neilia Hunter Biden: Joseph III, Robert, Naomi; with second wife Jill Biden: Ashley
PETS: Champ, Major, and Commander the German shepherds; Willow the gray tabby cat
EDUCATION: Attended Archmere Academy; Graduated from the University of Delaware (1965); Graduated from the College of Law- Syracuse University (1968)
RELIGION: Roman Catholic
OCCUPATION: Lawyer, public official
OTHER GOVERNMENT POSITIONS: U.S. Senator, 1973-2009; Vice President, 2009-17 (under Barack Obama)
MILITARY SERVICE: None
PRESIDENTIAL SALARY: $400,000/year + $50,000 expense account

Joe Biden

46th President of the United States (2021 –)

Joe Biden was raised in Scranton, Pennsylvania and Wilmington, Delaware, and grew up in a working-class family. He attended the University of Delaware and Syracuse Law School and became a lawyer. Joe Biden was elected to the U.S. Senate from Delaware in 1972, beginning his political career. He worked in the Senate for 36 years, where he was renowned for his work on foreign policy, crime prevention, and civil rights.

As Vice President under President Barack Obama, Biden played a key role in several accomplishments, including the passage of the Affordable Care Act, the economic stimulus package, and the Paris climate agreement. Biden was also a vocal advocate for LGBT rights and was instrumental in the repeal of "Don't Ask, Don't Tell," which banned openly gay people from serving in the military.

During his presidency, Biden has made several significant accomplishments. One of his first acts as President was to launch a comprehensive plan to combat the COVID-19 pandemic. The plan includes measures to increase vaccination rates, provide financial relief to those affected by the pandemic, and provide additional resources to schools and businesses.

Biden has also made significant progress in addressing climate change. He has re-joined the Paris climate agreement, canceled the Keystone XL pipeline, and announced plans to transition the country to 100% clean energy by 2035.

Besides these accomplishments, Biden has also made progress on several other fronts. He signed the American Rescue Plan, which provides relief to families and businesses affected by the pandemic, and he has taken steps to address systemic racism and inequality in the United States.

Overall, Joe Biden has had a long and successful career in public service, and significant accomplishments have already marked his presidency. As President, he has showed a commitment to addressing some of the most pressing issues facing the country today, and he has taken bold steps to move the United States forward.

Fun Facts:

- People have spotted Joe Biden enjoying a cone or two of ice cream in various places across the country.
- He has a stutter and has struggled with it since childhood. Biden has been open about his experience and has used it to connect with and inspire others who struggle with speech impediments.
- In 1972, shortly after being elected to the Senate, Biden's wife and infant daughter were killed in a car accident. His two sons were also in the car but survived. Officials swore Biden into the Senate at his sons' hospital bedside.
- Biden quotes poets, writes poetry, and owns Irish poetry.
- He has been known to be somewhat of a "space enthusiast" and has been a powerful advocate for NASA and space exploration. In fact, during his time as Vice President, Biden played a role in getting funding for NASA's Mars exploration program.
- Biden loves trains and often took Amtrak during his career. As a Senator, he commuted daily from Wilmington, Delaware to Washington, D.C. by train.

Chart of

Presidential Election Results

(1789 – present)

Election Year	Number of Presidency	Name of President and Political Party	Years of Office	Chief Opponents	Name of Vice President	Percentage of Popular Vote	Electoral Vote
1789	1st	George Washington (Unopposed)	1789-1797	N/A (Unopposed)	John Adams (1789-1797)	Unanimous electoral vote (100%)	69
1792		George Washington (Unopposed)	1793-1797	N/A (Unopposed)	John Adams (1789-1797)	Unanimous electoral vote (100%)	132
1796	2nd	John Adams (Federalist)	1797-1801	Thomas Jefferson (Democratic-Republican) Aaron Burr (Democratic-Republican)	Thomas Jefferson (1797-1801)	53.40%	71
1800	3rd	Thomas Jefferson (Democratic-Republican)	1801-1809	John Adams (Federalist) Charles Cotesworth Pinckney (Federalist) Aaron Burr (Democratic-Republican)	Aaron Burr (1801–1805) George Clinton (1805–1809)	61.40%	73
1804		Thomas Jefferson (Democratic-Republican) (Unopposed)	1805-1809	N/A (Unopposed)	George Clinton (1805–1809)	N/A	176
1808	4th	James Madison (Democratic-Republican)	1809-1817	Charles Cotesworth Pinckney (Federalist) DeWitt Clinton (Democratic-Republican)	George Clinton (1809–1812) Elbridge Gerry (1813–1814)	64.70%	122
1812		James Madison (Democratic-Republican)	1813-1817	DeWitt Clinton (Federalist)	Elbridge Gerry (1813–1814) vacant (1814–1817)	50.40%	128
1816	5th	James Monroe (Democratic-Republican) (Unopposed)	1817-1825	N/A (Unopposed)	Daniel D. Tompkins (1817–1825)	N/A	183
1820		James Monroe (Democratic-Republican) (Unopposed)	1821-1825	N/A (Unopposed)	Daniel D. Tompkins (1817–1825)	N/A	231
1824	6th	John Quincy Adams (Democratic-Republican/National Republican)	1825-1829	Andrew Jackson (Democratic-Republican) William H. Crawford (Democratic-Republican) Henry Clay (National Republican)	John C. Calhoun (1825–1832)	30.90%	84
1828	7th	Andrew Jackson (Democratic)	1829-1837	John Quincy Adams (National Republican)	John C. Calhoun (1829–1832) Martin Van Buren (1833–1837)	56.00%	178
1832		Andrew Jackson (Democratic)	1833-1837	Henry Clay (National Republican) John Floyd (Nullifier) William Wirt (Anti-Masonic)	Martin Van Buren (1833–1837)	54.70%	219
1836	8th	Martin Van Buren (Democratic)	1837-1841	William Henry Harrison (Whig) Hugh Lawson White (Whig) Daniel Webster (Whig)	Richard M. Johnson (1837–1841)	50.80%	170
1840	9th	William Henry Harrison (Whig)	1841	Martin Van Buren (Democratic)	John Tyler (1841)	52.90%	234
	10th	John Tyler	1841-1845		None		

Election Year	Number of Presidency	Name of President and Political Party	Years of Office	Chief Opponents	Name of Vice President	Percentage of Popular Vote	Electoral Vote
1844	11th	James K. Polk (Democratic)	1845-1849	Henry Clay (Whig)	George M. Dallas (1845–1849)	49.50%	170
1848	12th	Zachary Taylor (Whig)	1849-1850	Lewis Cass (Democratic) Martin Van Buren (Free Soil)	Millard Fillmore (1849–1850)	47.30%	163
1852	14th	Franklin Pierce (Democratic)	1853-1857	Winfield Scott (Whig) John P. Hale (Free Soil)	William R. King (1853)	50.80%	254
1856	15th	James Buchanan (Democratic)	1857-1861	John C. Frémont (Republican) Millard Fillmore (American)	John C. Breckinridge (1857–1861)	45.30%	174
1860	16th	Abraham Lincoln (Republican)	1861-1865	John C. Breckinridge (Southern Democratic) John Bell (Constitutional Union) Stephen A. Douglas (Northern Democratic)	Hannibal Hamlin (1861–1865)	39.80%	180
1864		Abraham Lincoln (National Union)	1865-1869	George B. McClellan (Democratic)	Andrew Johnson (1865–1869)	55.00%	212
	17th	Andrew Johnson (Democrat)	1865-1869		None		
1868	18th	Ulysses S. Grant (Republican)	1869-1877	Horatio Seymour (Democratic)	Schuyler Colfax (1869–1873) Henry Wilson (1873–1875)	52.70%	214
1872		Ulysses S. Grant (Republican)	1873-1877	Horace Greeley (Democratic) B. Gratz Brown (Liberal Republican)	Henry Wilson (1873–1875) vacant (1875–1877)	55.60%	286
1876	19th	Rutherford B. Hayes (Republican)	1877-1881	Samuel J. Tilden (Democratic)	William A. Wheeler (1877–1881)	47.90%	185
1880	20th	James A. Garfield (Republican)	1881	Winfield S. Hancock (Democratic)	Chester A. Arthur (1881)	48.30%	214
	21st	Chester A. Arthur (Republican)	1881-1885				
1884	22nd	Grover Cleveland (Democratic)	1885-1889	James G. Blaine (Republican)	Thomas A. Hendricks (1885)	48.90%	219
1888	23rd	Benjamin Harrison (Republican)	1889-1893	Grover Cleveland (Democratic)	Levi P. Morton (1889–1893)	47.80%	233
1892	24th	Grover Cleveland (Democratic)	1893-1897	Benjamin Harrison (Republican) James B. Weaver (Populist)	Adlai E. Stevenson I (1893–1897)	46.00%	277
1896	25th	William McKinley (Republican)	1897-1901	William Jennings Bryan (Democratic Populist)	Garret A. Hobart (1897–1899) Theodore Roosevelt (1901)	51.00%	271
1900		William McKinley (Republican)	1901	William Jennings Bryan (Democratic)	Theodore Roosevelt (1901)	51.60%	292
	26th	Theodore Roosevelt (Republican)	1901-1905		None		
1904		Theodore Roosevelt (Republican)	1905-1909	Alton B. Parker (Democratic)	Charles W. Fairbanks (1905–1909)	56.40%	336
1908	27th	William Howard Taft (Republican)	1909-1913	William Jennings Bryan (Democratic)	James S. Sherman (1909–1912) vacant (1912–1913)	51.60%	321
1912	28th	Woodrow Wilson (Democratic)	1913-1921	William Howard Taft (Republican) Theodore Roosevelt (Progressive)	Thomas R. Marshall (1913–1921)	41.80%	435
1916		Woodrow Wilson (Democratic)	1917-1921	Charles E. Hughes (Republican)	Thomas R. Marshall (1917–1921)	49.20%	277
1920	29th	Warren G. Harding (Republican)	1921-1923	James M. Cox (Democratic)	Calvin Coolidge (1921–1923)	60.30%	404
	30th	Calvin Coolidge (Republican)	1923-1925		None		
1924		Calvin Coolidge (Republican)	1925-1929	John W. Davis (Democratic) Robert M. La Follette Sr. (Progressive)	Charles G. Dawes (1925–1929)	54.00%	382
1928	31st	Herbert Hoover (Republican)	1929-1933	Al Smith (Democratic)	Charles Curtis (1929–1933)	58.20%	444
1932	32nd	Franklin D. Roosevelt (Democratic)	1933-1945	Herbert Hoover (Republican)	John Nance Garner (1933–1941) Henry A. Wallace (1941–1945) Harry S. Truman (1945)	57.40%	472
1936		Franklin D. Roosevelt (Democratic)	1937-1945	Alf Landon (Republican)	John Nance Garner (1937–1941) Henry A. Wallace (1941–1945) Harry S. Truman (1945)	60.80%	523

Election Year	Number of Presidency	Name of President and Political Party	Years of Office	Chief Opponents	Name of Vice President	Percentage of Popular Vote	Electoral Vote
1940		Franklin D. Roosevelt (Democratic)	1941-1945	Wendell Willkie (Republican)	Henry A. Wallace (1941–1945) Harry S. Truman (1945)	54.70%	449
1944		Franklin D. Roosevelt (Democratic)	1945-1949†	Thomas E. Dewey (Republican)	Harry S. Truman (1945–1949†)	53.40%	432
	33rd	Harry S. Truman (Democrat)	1944-1949				
1948		Harry S. Truman (Democratic)	1949-1953	Thomas E. Dewey (Republican) Strom Thurmond (Dixiecrat)	Alben W. Barkley (1949–1953)	49.60%	303
1952	34th	Dwight D. Eisenhower (Republican)	1953-1961	Adlai Stevenson II (Democratic)	Richard Nixon (1953–1961)	55.20%	442
1956		Dwight D. Eisenhower (Republican)	1957-1961	Adlai Stevenson II (Democratic)	Richard Nixon (1957–1961)	57.40%	457
1960	35th	John F. Kennedy (Democratic)	1961-1963†	Richard Nixon (Republican)	Lyndon B. Johnson (1961–1963†)	49.70%	303
	36th	Lyndon B. Johnson (Democrat)	1963-1964		None		
1964		Lyndon B. Johnson (Democratic)	1965-1969†	Barry Goldwater (Republican)	Hubert Humphrey (1965–1969†)	61.10%	486
1968	37th	Richard Nixon (Republican)	1969-1974†	Hubert Humphrey (Democratic) George Wallace (American Independent)	Spiro Agnew (1969–1973†) Gerald Ford (1973–1974†)	43.40%	301
1972		Richard Nixon (Republican)	1973-1974†	George McGovern (Democratic)	Spiro Agnew (1973†) Gerald Ford (1973–1974†)	60.70%	520
	38th	Gerald R. Ford (Democrat)	1974-1977				
1976	39th	Jimmy Carter (Democratic)	1977-1981	Gerald Ford (Republican)	Walter Mondale (1977–1981)	50.10%	297
1980	40th	Ronald Reagan (Republican)	1981-1989	Jimmy Carter (Democratic)	George H. W. Bush (1981–1989)	50.70%	489
1984		Ronald Reagan (Republican)	1985-1989	Walter Mondale (Democratic)	George H. W. Bush (1985–1989)	58.80%	525
1988	41st	George H. W. Bush (Republican)	1989-1993	Michael Dukakis (Democratic)	Dan Quayle (1989–1993)	53.40%	426
1992	42nd	Bill Clinton (Democratic)	1993-2001	George H. W. Bush (Republican) Ross Perot (Independent)	Al Gore (1993–2001)	43.00%	370
1996		Bill Clinton (Democratic)	1997-2001	Bob Dole (Republican) Ross Perot (Reform)	Al Gore (1997–2001)	49.20%	379
2000	43rd	George W. Bush (Republican)	2001-2009	Al Gore (Democratic)	Dick Cheney (2001–2009)	47.90%	271
2004		George W. Bush (Republican)	2005-2009	John Kerry (Democratic)	Dick Cheney (2005–2009)	50.70%	286
2008	44th	Barack Obama (Democratic)	2009-2017	John McCain (Republican)	Joe Biden (2009–2017)	52.90%	365
2012		Barack Obama (Democratic)	2013-2017	Mitt Romney (Republican)	Joe Biden (2013–2017)	51.10%	332
2016	45th	Donald Trump (Republican)	2017-2021†	Hillary Clinton (Democratic)	Mike Pence (2017–2021†)	46.10%	304
2020	46th	Joe Biden	2021-	Donald Trump	Kamala Harris (2021–)	51.30%	306

Resource Guide

BOOKS:
Barber, James David. *Presidents.* DK Children, 2000.

DeGregorio, William A. *The Complete Book of U.S. Presidents*. Random House, 1993.

Gutman, Dan. *The Kid Who Ran for President*. Paw Prints, 2012.

Meltzer, Brad. *I am* series (e.g., *I am George Washington, I am Abraham Lincoln*). New York: Dial Books.

Who Was series by various authors (e.g., *Who Was George Washington?*, *Who Was Abraham Lincoln?*). New York: Penguin Workshop.

VIDEOS:
The American Presidents documentary series by PBS. Directed by Philip B. Kunhardt III, Nancy Steiner, and Michael Epstein. Produced by Kunhardt Films. 1995.

Presidents of the United States videos on YouTube by Homeschool Pop. Homeschool Pop, 2018.

Crash Course U.S. History videos on YouTube by John Green (Episodes on the U.S. Presidents). Crash Course, 2013.

Liberty's Kids animated series (Episodes on the Revolutionary War and founding of the nation). PBS Kids, 2002.

TELEVISION PROGRAMS:
Presidential Libraries: America's Presidents on C-SPAN. C-SPAN, 2007.

The Presidents on the History Channel. Directed by Matthew Ginsburg. Produced by Brook Lapping Productions and History Channel. 2005.

The American President on the Discovery Channel. Directed by William K. Wolfrum. Produced by KPI Productions and Discovery Channel. 2000.

The West Wing (TV series). Created by Aaron Sorkin. NBC, 1999-2006.

PLACES TO VISIT:
Mount Rushmore National Memorial. Keystone, South Dakota.

Washington D.C. (White House, National Archives, Smithsonian Museums).

Presidential Libraries and Museums (e.g., the Ronald Reagan Presidential Library, the Abraham Lincoln Presidential Library and Museum, etc.).

Independence Hall and the Liberty Bell in Philadelphia.

WEBSITES:
The White House website (www.whitehouse.gov).

The National Park Service website (www.nps.gov) for information on presidential landmarks and memorials.

The Miller Center at the University of Virginia (millercenter.org) for resources on the U.S. presidency and public policy.

The History Channel website (www.history.com) for articles and videos on U.S. presidents and history.

Bibliography

Beschloss, Michael R. *Presidential Courage: Brave Leaders and How They Changed America 1789-1989*. Simon and Schuster, 2008.

DeGregorio, William A. *The Complete Book of U.S. Presidents*. Random House, 1993.

Genovese, Michael A., et al. *Presidency and Domestic Policy: Comparing Leadership Styles, FDR to Obama*. Routledge, 2015.

Gormley, Ken. *The Presidents and the Constitution: A Living History*. NYU Press, 2016.

Graff, Henry. *The Presidents: A Reference History*. Scribners, 1997.

Jones, Charles O. *The American Presidency: A Very Short Introduction*. Oxford UP, 2016.

---. *The Presidency in a Separated System*. Rowman and Littlefield, 2000.

Matuz, Roger. *The Presidents Fact Book: A Comprehensive Handbook to the Achievements, Powers, and History of Every President from George Washington to Donald Trump*. Black Dog & Leventhal, 2016.

Milkis, Sidney M., and Michael Nelson. *The American Presidency: A Historical and Contemporary Analysis*. CQ Press, 2022.

Milkis, Sidney M. *The President and the Parties: The Transformation of the American Party System Since the New Deal*. Oxford UP, 1993.

Moore, Kathryn. *The American President: A Complete History*. Union Square, 2018

Nelson, Michael L. "The Presidency A to Z." *Congressional Quarterly*, Jan. 2003.

Philosophy, Brian Duignan Senior Editor Religion And. *The Executive Branch of the Federal Government: Purpose, Process, and People*. The Rosen Publishing Group, Inc, 2009.

"Presidential Pet Museum." Presidential Pet Museum, 2016, Www.presidentialpetmuseum.com/.

"Presidents of the United States | Ipl: Information You Can Trust." Www.ipl.org, www.ipl.org/div/potus/.

Skowronek, Stephen. "Presidential Leadership in Political Time: Reprise and Reappraisal." *Choice Reviews Online*, vol. 46, no. 02, Association of College and Research Libraries, Oct. 2008, pp. 46–1175. https://doi.org/10.5860/choice.46-1175.

Whitney, David. *The American Presidents: Biographies of the Chief Executives from George Washington to Barack Obama.* Reader's Digest, 2012.

About Mike Black

Mike Black has a passion for history and a talent for making it accessible to young readers. His engaging books bring the past to life with vivid storytelling and carefully researched details.

Mike has always been fascinated by history and the stories of the people who lived in different times and places. He believes that learning about the past can help us better understand the world we live in today, and that history can be fun and exciting when presented in the right way.

Through his books, Mike strives to spark a love of history in young readers and inspire them to learn more about the world around them. He believes that every child deserves the opportunity to explore the past and discover the fascinating stories of the people who came before us.

www.ingramcontent.com/pod-product-compliance
Lightning Source LLC
LaVergne TN
LVHW061253100826
845148LV00008B/1113